MW01144626

Designed by the Master:
Women of Permeating Influence

K. Ellen Jacobs

PRESS

Printed in the United States of America
www.xulonpress.com

ISBN 978-1-60791-689-5

Cover photograph by Jonalee Castruccio.
Authors photograph by Palmer's Studio.

Dearest Renee!
Many blessings
on you as you read
the stories of these ladies!
Continue to spread His
fragrance everywhere.

Love,
Ellen Jacobs
2 Cor 2:14-15

In memory of my Grams for her Christ-like character, unconditional love and sweet influence. To my precious daughters Jackie, Daneen and Susan for enriching my life; they are my pride and joy. Finally, to my Lord and the women He placed in my life, for they all have taught me much.

Introduction

The Lord impressed this project upon my heart about five years ago, and I am amazed at how the Lord brought it to completion. First, He designed the lives of these women so that sharing their stories would encourage and point to the true solution for all their circumstances, Jesus Christ. Most of all, He helped me through many tears and much heartache as I relived the early seasons of my own life. Each intimate, telling story shows the Lord's grace and tender mercies bestowed and received by those that were, as we all are, undeserving. All my praise and gratitude goes to such a wonderful, loving and caring God who finishes what He starts.

So many women have had input in a variety of ways that this almost no longer feels like my own work. I offer a big thank you to these ten women who contributed their stories (some of whose names have been changed to protect their identity). My heartfelt gratitude to Karen Willoughby whose love, expertise and wise encouragement helped me to begin and to continue until this work was completed. In addition, for their expertise in the editing process, I give a big shout of thanks to Gerry Thompson, Tara Cox, Shari Stidd, Gina Weigand and Tina Brown. Many thanks to Darci Harder for obtaining the services of a friend for the book cover. Their hard work brought this work to its conclusion.

My deepest thanks also go to my dear friends Chris Hill and Laurie Smith, who kept a pulse not only on this work, but also on me. Their love, laughter, heart and prayers will go with me to heaven where we will meet again.

To my family at Salem Heights Church, and to my pastors and elders who make it possible for an older woman like me to serve as part of a vibrant and relevant ministry – I thank you too! Finally, I must recognize my friend and boss at Corban College, Rich (Dr. Richard Meyers, Psy.D.), who always saw my potential and possibilities even though I felt unsure and inadequate. For the blessing of such brothers and sisters in the Lord, my heart is full of abundant joy.

I do not know if I'll take on the challenge of writing another book in the future, but I do know there are more stories to search for and tell. Therefore, I will trust the Lord to do what He desires.

Ellen — Graceful

Romans 8:29; 2 Corinthians 5:17; Ephesians
2:8; Colossians 3:10; Titus 2:1-6

I'm an old lady who ought to be in a convalescent home, mental hospital or wheelchair. However, thanks to God's kindness, I am still functioning and in the ministry He so graciously gave me thirty-three years ago. I have mainly ministered to women; and in serving them, one ongoing trait has caused me great sadness: many women tend to think of themselves as inferior or as second-class citizens. According to the Scriptures, there are no — I repeat — no second class-citizens in God's economy. I encounter women, both Christian and not, young and old, thick and thin, married and single, size two to size twenty-two, who have bought into the lie of the Evil One regarding their role and their worth. This lie pervades our culture, and too often, many churches and even marriages. All women ought to think rightly about the person the Master Designer created them to be. That is my heartfelt desire for all women, but especially for those that read this book. In John 17:17, we are told what truth is able to do: *"Sanctify them in truth; Thy word is truth"* (Italics mine).

Within the deepest recesses of my being, is the hope that my life leaves a legacy of godly change behind. Moreover, I hope my character and attitude is as attractive and wears as nicely as the clothes I put on each morning.

Before coming to Christ, that lie permeated my being. Every negative circumstance that transpired from my childhood until I came to know Christ supported and paid credence to that lie. At times, when we believe something, even though it is untrue, we internally substantiate that untruth. This happened to me. However, Scripture is very clear: *"…the truth shall make you free…"* (John 8:31-38, Italics mine). When a woman believes the Scriptures and sees herself through the eyes of her Creator, transformation and a rewiring of her thought processes takes place. Through this process of change, each woman who believed the lie that devalued her sense of worth can learn to debunk it. Then she can shout with boldness the truth, "Because of Christ, I am not a second-class citizen!"

But let me start at the beginning. I was the only girl, born into a family with three living brothers. A couple of months before my delivery, my oldest brother drowned, a tragedy Mom was never able to reconcile. One moment she had a vibrant, energetic young boy; then, while still in the throes of grief and after a tough delivery, comes a sickly girl – not exactly a fair exchange. However, like good Germans, the family pulled up their proverbial bootstraps and moved forward – that is, everyone but Mom. The loss left her with a gaping hole in her heart, still bleeding for her lost boy. Mom never recovered.

Ironically, the time of my brother's death and my birth, was during the Great Depression. Our family lived in a small town in the Pacific Northwest. Dad found work wherever he could. Mom tried her best to keep our family and home intact. I remember Dad worked for a short time at a nursery, and instead of bringing home a paycheck, he brought home plants. Mom was extremely angry. During those horrible months, Mom had charged groceries at a small local grocery store. When the creditor wanted to be paid, Mom turned over her prized possession — her piano — in order to clear the debt. I am sure that she resented this turn of events as she had worked extremely hard for the piano before she married Dad. Now, the only time Mom would be able to see it was when she walked by the grocer's home — for it was visible through the bay window. After some time went by, she stopped walking by his home — the pain was too great. Apparently, this issue went unresolved for Mom because it would unexpectedly creep into other conversations.

When I was about four years old, a curious thing happened. I saw Mom in the kitchen counting her jars of home-canned fruits and vegetables that had been in the pantry. She counted out to ten then set one aside. Apparently, from what I could understand, these jars were their tithe to the church. It was Christmas time and times were hard. As she counted out the jars, she encountered a dilemma. (In truth, we were not

Christians, even though we occasionally attended the Methodist church where Mom had taught Sunday school at one time). I do not remember the outcome of that quandary, but I do remember going with both Mom and Dad to the church one night. Due to the following event that transpired that evening, a desire for the Lord began flickering in my heart. This stirring, I later discovered was the beginning of a quest for Him and His grace. However, much heartache and thousands of lies would get in the way before that quest would become a reality.

On this particular Christmas, while my parents were talking with the minister, I went into the sanctuary and saw the Nativity scene; I was drawn to it. I went and knelt at the manger. I am not sure how long I stayed lost in the wonder of the scene, seeing Jesus lying in that tiny bed. Dad's yell startled me and pulled me back to reality; it was time to leave. Running after Dad, I looked back giddy after my encounter with Jesus yelling at the top of my lungs, "Happy Birthday, Jesus!" From that moment on, a thirst within my soul began which went unsatisfied for another thirty-six years.

Three years later, life began to change for our family. Newspapers, magazines and newsreels at the movie theaters talked non-stop of one thing: World War II. The picture I remember most, though, is a memory of the war at home and the night my parents decided to divorce.

I was about seven on that fateful evening Mother came running into my room and sat on the side of the bed. I woke up and saw her crying. I was startled and scared. Mom spoke softly, reassuring me all would be well. However, in my heart, and in the pit of my stomach, I knew things were not well. As I cried, she held me. Within moments, Dad entered my room, pulled the dressing table chair out, swung it around so that the back was facing him and he sat down. Dad looked serious and sad. He said, "I guess this means it's over." Mom nodded her head up and down, indicating a yes. With that, Dad turned and left the house. Mom again tried to reassure me, but something in my heart told me that this event would change my life forever.

The next day when I came home from school, upon opening our front door, my eyes saw a big leather box — it was a suitcase. This was the first time I had ever seen one. Dad must have seen the shock and fear on my face because he pulled me into his strong arms and held me tightly. My little body shook as I cried uncontrollably. I may have been only a child, but somehow I sensed again that my life would never be the same. Dad tried to calm me down by speaking softly, trying to reassure me that he loved me and all would be well; somehow, I knew differently. That is the first time Dad ever lied to me.

Then, just before he left the house, he handed me a small white box, like a restaurant take-out box. Excitedly, I opened it up to find a turtle inside. After four months, the turtle's shell turned soft. I thought he had died, so I buried him in the little white box amongst the bushes that we had received months before in lieu of a paycheck. Later, I learned the turtle probably was not dead, but rather hibernating. Hearing that news, I ran outside to dig him up, but all I found was an empty white box. My turtle was gone just like my dad. Again, tears began to stream down my face, realizing that both Dad and my turtle were gone forever.

By this time, in 1943, one brother was in the Navy serving in the South Seas and another worked at a government ship building plant. Mom went to work in an airplane factory. Dad had moved north and built warships; he was a welder. The divorce decree gave him visitation rights to see me and my brother once a month.

Tragedy struck our family again shortly after the divorce. My youngest brother had a horrible accident and severely burned his leg. The doctor treated him at home until his leg became so badly infected that the doctor, fearing for his life, put him in the hospital. He spent almost a year in the hospital and underwent multiple skin graft surgeries. In those days, they did "pinch grafts." As I recall this event, they had to use restraints to hold him down and used some type of a tool for pinch grafting. They took the inched flesh from his thighs and buttocks and used it to fill in the holes of his burned flesh. It is hard to imagine the mental and physical trauma he went through. Unfortunately, he returned home a different boy than I had known before.

Physically, he came home healed. However, the scars on his leg mirrored the scars on his mind and soul from the pain and trauma of that horrible experience. Who remained was someone I did not know and learned to fear. My brother experienced a major personality change. Pain can often be as permanently debilitating to a child's heart and mind as any physical wound left behind. Looking back, it seems as if tragedy was a big part of my life and my family's life — the war, divorce, the accident, neglect and abuse; one following after the other.

All of those incidences created confusion and a deep loneliness within me. I, like my brother, was never the same. Looking back, I now realize I was clinically depressed, but in those days, no one seemed to know about depression or its symptoms. Moreover, no one had time or the inclination to pay attention to a sad, lonely kid. I do believe Mom tried. For a short while, Mom read books to us in the evening — books like *My Friend Flicka* and *Huckleberry Finn*. That special time was short lived, however, as Mom began to date and go dancing every Saturday night, leaving us to either stay home alone, have the neighbor boy watch us or sleep at one of her friend's houses.

Not surprising, Mom had her own set of issues to deal with and attempted to find various and unhealthy ways to soothe them. Her quest for relief from her pain left no time for me or my brother, who was also in pain; his was physical and emotional while mine was emotional. We had to fend for ourselves as best as we could. So, what does a child of seven do with her feelings? Too often, we cope as best as we can with our limited capacity to understand. We each try to find some way to soothe our pain. For me, it was a world of fantasy — watching movies or listening to the radio. The highlight of my day was immersing myself in the radio serials like *The Lone Ranger*. Then, at night, we listened to mystery programs like *Inner Sanctum*.

My mom's way of escape was drinking, men, dancing and later, pills. My form of self-medication was movies and singing songs of the 1940's. Most of the music, during the war, was sorrowful and somehow seemed to give me permission to feel bad and cry. Unfortunately, there seemed to be no end to the sadness, loneliness and crying. Those emotions created a desperate need, almost an insatiable need, to be with people — anybody would do. There is little doubt in my mind that those feelings and need for human closeness and interaction exacerbated my loneliness. Those needs probably became the driving force in my becoming the neighborhood nuisance, who was always knocking on someone's door. I was never home unless I had to be.

Children left adrift without caring supervision, no one to listen to their heart and a lack of direction, unfortunately, will devise their own ways to cope. For my youngest brother and me, we skipped school and took up smoking. My weekend escape was movies — especially George Raft movies because he resembled my dad. However, these movies only caused to deepen the loneliness for Dad, which led to more crying. Looking back, my eyes must have been red and swollen most of the time. Yet, no one asked what was wrong. Parents too often become myopic; caught up in their own pain and unable to see their own children hurting and feeling left out.

It seemed that everyone was focused on the war and trying to make the best out of a bad situation. Mom was no different. Mom, like so many other lonely women, married and unmarried, found dancing and drinking as an escape from the uncertainty of the day. Not surprisingly, Mom's absenteeism seemed to exacerbate my issues of fear, insecurities, sleeping problems and crying myself to sleep most nights.

As I reflect back on my life, I thank God for His grace, which He meted out to a lonely, bewildered, troublemaking seven year old. For in the absence of a godly, nurturing mother, God raised up other women who taught and modeled how a woman ought to behave and how she should live long before I belonged to Him. The lessons they taught were always within my heart and mind, but bore no fruit until years later.

My grandmother was one of those women which I will share about in length a bit later; she became the most important adult in my life. From her I learned the value of family, home, faith and country and the importance of my marriage vows. Until her stroke and eventual death, she taught me many invaluable lessons. Some of those lessons still live on today in my personal and professional life.

God's graceful intervention on my life also included two special neighbors: Clara and Halla. Clara lived next door, and had two girls and two boys. We played together a lot. Clara was a Norwegian from North Dakota. They often spoke in their native tongue when they did not want others to know what they were saying. As a nosy little girl, I found this disconcerting. Nevertheless, Clara's heart was made of gold. She helped my mom by doing her laundry, tended to me when I had earaches, talked with me, and even scolded me — chastising me through words of disappointment or a stern look. Her corrections were well-intended and, unfortunately, needed often. However, I never got upset with her. I am sure that she would not say the same about me, but she was gracious.

She and her family attended church regularly and their minister often visited unannounced. (I can remember one time her kids and I were playing cards when he stopped by. As soon as we heard he was out front, we hustled to get those cards out of sight and then sat like angels through his visit.) Clara was a class "A" mom and a good friend to me as well. Even when I got older, I would visit with her on occasion, though more and more infrequently as time went on. I regret now that I never shared with her how her life had impacted me. When I would come home early from elementary school with an earache, she would come over and nurse me tenderly by her soft words, pats on the head and the warm melted butter she pored in my ear for relief. On many occasions instead of coming home to a cold, empty house, Clara would be there washing our clothes. Clara was much like Christ, a refuge from the concern and pain of life during the hard years after WWII.

Halla also made a deep impression on a lonely, scared, neighborhood waif. She lived right behind our house. If you have seen June Cleaver from the classic show *Leave it to Beaver,* then you have the perfect image of Halla. She wore starched house-dresses and high heels. She was tidy, soft-spoken, and loved to entertain the neighbor ladies who stayed at home and attended to their daily chores of house and family.

Once a month, all the neighborhood women got together for tea, gossip and to share recipes. During the 1940's, these get-togethers were called coffee klatches. I can remember being present at one and watching the hostess, Halla, use a silver teaspoon when serving tea. When I inquired why, she said it would keep the china cup from cracking. Her home was not just a house — but a home. With a gracious and gentle spirit, she built into her children — and even me — a sense of purpose and belonging. Halla's beauty grew from her moral and righteous behavior; she glowed from the inside out.

Halla's husband, Shorty, worked every year in Alaska, and I do not remember much about him. I do recall a particular day when he was home for which I am grateful. My brother stormed over to their house very angry and seemingly out of control. He pounded on their front door, and when Halla answered, he asked for me. I went gingerly to the front door after Halla called me and he grabbed my arm, attempting to yank me out of their house, yelling that I needed to come home. Scared and feeling terror welling up within me, I screamed — knowing what would take place if I did go with him. I told him that I did not want to go home until our mother came home from work. He persisted and Shorty came to the door and yelled at him to go home. Shorty's intervention saved me, at least for that day.

No one, outside of God and my brother, knew the daily dread I lived with. No one knew my home was not safe. Abuse can come in many forms — neglect, sexual, physical, emotional and psychological — all of which I experienced from age four until fourteen. Either my mom did not see the signs of abuse, or because she was dealing with her own set of demons, she unfortunately and hopefully unwittingly neglected me. Some of my male family members took advantage of me. Not only is this hard to relive, but it is also hard for those who have not experienced such a horror to understand the daily terror and its lasting effects. Dr. Dan Allender in his book, *The Wounded Heart,* states that abuse damages a person's soul. Abuse causes children and adults to have a distorted view of themselves, life in general, as well as the living God. Distortions regarding our personhood can change when we know the truth. Although our scars remain, they are no longer debilitating, but a constant reminder of His healing grace. Those scars now can shine as stars for His glory. His power and grace is a demonstration that He alone is able to do such a great work. He is the only One who can heal the inner man, and all honor and praise belong to Him.

I will always hold a deep gratitude for the moms in our neighborhood. In my chaotic world, they gave me a taste of normal life and a realization that it was possible. This was especially important when I felt waves of deep despair. This is my tribute to Grams, Clara and Halla — and many other wonderful women — whose lives created a permeating aroma, like a perfume that filled the air as they walked through my life. These pillars of femininity influenced me then, and continue to this day.

Unfortunately, today we see an abundance of two-career families, leaving many youngsters at home alone or at a daycare center. These are helpful, but the children miss out on having stay-at-home moms as neighbors who can offer a place of comfort and refuge. Children like me, who don't have the opportunity to see what a healthy family looks like, need loving neighbors to allow them into their home and experience a different, healthy environment. This can instill hope for their future as it did for me. Too many little children live in abusive homes with wounded souls. I pray that God will bring a teacher, pastor or concerned parent into their lives to be a positive influence on them, the way He did for me.

There is little worth sharing about my teen years that would edify or build up another. (A couple high-lights would include my visits to one of my aunt's — sometimes for a whole week. Another highlight I remember occurred during a family outing when my Aunt Opal carried me on her back while she was dancing to the "Beer Barrel Polka". Beyond that there is no more to tell).

Because of my tumultuous childhood, I will sum up those years in a few statements: I dated early, got married at the delicate age of fifteen and had three wonderful girls who have blessed my life. My marriage lasted twenty-five years. Some years were good and some not so good. Although both Gordon and I were raised in the same denomination and had a sense of God; neither of us had a real relationship with Christ. I am grateful that God had better plans for us.

My journey towards a relationship with Christ began with Lela, or Lee, as I call her. We worked together at Zonolite, a manufacturing plant that made insulation. I ran forced-air mold machines and packaged the materials it made. One fateful afternoon they called me to work. We had only enough food in the house for a half tuna fish sandwich. As we broke for lunch, Lee asked, "Is that all you have?" I turned away crying and embarrassed, and softly muttered, "That is all we had."

That night Darlene (Lee's sister) and her husband arrived at our house. They brought in two big bags of groceries and a five-dollar bill. They visited with us and shared that they both had come to Christ about a year earlier. Then, unexpectedly, they invited Gordon and me to a Bible study. So, we went. It was not well organized, but the people were great and prayed for my family and our situation. We attended that whole summer, and the leader shared with the group how to accept Christ. Suddenly, the search I began as a child at a Christmas manger began to have a destination.

Because of Lee and that unorganized Bible study, I accepted Jesus (though not as my Lord and Savior) because I wanted Him to rescue me from my circumstances rather than from my sin. Still spiritually unsatisfied, my search continued even stronger than before for a resolution to my inner turmoil. I began to see my need, but it was as if I was seeing truth through a dark mirror. I prayed fervently for God to fill that emptiness I had felt my whole life. I tried reading the Scriptures, but they made no sense. I cried, "Get me out of this mess!"

Two years later, God answered my cry as He led me to another Bible study where, for the first time in my life, I understood that Jesus Christ loved me and died for my sins. He desired that I come to Him just as I was, all my warts and scars included. All I had to do was believe that He died for me and accept that free gift. I did not need to remake myself first — nor do you, dear reader — in order for God to accept you. As I carefully studied the Bible, I could see my need to have my sin eradicated, and I could see that Jesus was the only One who could do that. Collapsing on my bedroom floor in grief over what Christ had done on Calvary's cross for me because of my sin, I surrendered.

I had been married for twenty-four years when I came to Christ in February of 1975. That first year as a truly committed believer felt akin to entering spiritual kindergarten. Women entered my Christian life and God used them to help me grow.

One of those women God used was Wanetta Young. She and her husband Darrell had prayed for ten years that my husband and I would come to Christ. Darrell was my husband's best friend. Darrell and Gordon worked at the same company and played softball, bowled and fished together. I jokingly have said at times that God broke their new television set so they would end up at my home that fateful Monday evening; I was at the end of my rope and had no place left to run, except to Christ. Wanetta was Christ's ambassador.

Wanetta attended BSF (Bible Study Fellowship) and had invited me years prior to that evening, but I declined to go because it sounded too religious for me. However, that night "too religious" did not sound too bad. Gordon had just had his third heart attack, which left him completely disabled. He could not continue to work at his job, and after he had been out of work for a year, all our resources were spent. I had come to the end of my own strength, looking fearfully into the future that would not include my husband of twenty-five years. When Wanetta and Darrell showed up at our house to watch a football game, I asked her in bold desperation if she still attended BSF and if I could go as well. She agreed, and we arranged to go together to an introduction class starting that same week. I was excited and scared at the same time.

When I entered the church, I was overwhelmed to see more than four hundred women sitting in the pews. I was awestruck by how beautiful they were. It was not just their physical beauty; it was a beauty that came from inside. I came to see and understand it was the beauty of Christ shining through them. The leader asked us to write on the back of the attendance sheet why we wanted to be a part of this study. I wrote, "I want to know more about God." Even though I felt ill equipped, I was able to get into a class. The study was on the Book of Matthew. I did not understand at the time what a divine placement this group would be.

I was thrilled when I received a call from Donna, a discussion leader who invited me to attend her class.

Donna was a wonderful, gentle woman who loved the Lord and His Word. I believe that God chose her specifically to touch my life.

When our little group had its monthly luncheon, I was very nervous. After all, these were godly women, and I was a person with little exposure to delicate hospitality and manners. Being my nervous self, I grabbed for my cigarettes and lit one up as I looked for an ashtray. No ashtray was in sight! I am glad I missed the looks of surprise on Donna and the host's face. I was so insecure that had the women made a fuss, I would have left and never gone back. Nevertheless, thanks to the Holy Spirit's work in their lives, they paid no attention to my smoking and went on with the luncheon. I am deeply grateful for Donna's maturity in Christ and her acceptance of a waif needing spiritual discipleship and love, both of which she gave abundantly. I remain, however, mortified at my lack of social grace.

Through God's grace, I learned to trust Him in the years that followed. The more I trusted Him, the more control I let Him have in my life. In addition, as I studied the Bible, and grew in its knowledge, I discovered how distorted my previous view of life and God was because of my experiences. The Bible gave me a new way to think and live. God still uses His Word to mold and shape me into the image of Jesus.

As my relationship with God grew, He placed in my heart an insatiable appetite for the Scriptures. I could not study it enough. I would take home my weekly lesson and do all five days in about two hours. I cherished my time with Him. In order to do my studying, I rose early or stayed up late depending on what was happening at home. My husband, two girls and a grandson who lived with us, began to see a different person.

Implementing what I learned from the Scriptures, I began to submit to my husband, to love him deeper and saw our marriage with a different purpose. I worked for Zonolite full-time for a period, but as I came to understand God's role for me as a wife, I began to work only on an on-call basis. On another occasion, I surprised Gordy by returning his biblical role of husband and leader, especially when it came to parenting our youngest daughter. He then surprised *me* by doing a great job. I wondered, "Why did I wait so long?"

My family saw the changes, (probably because they were extreme), in both my demeanor and approach to life with all of its demands and uncertainties. My youngest girl said after a particular harrowing time, "Mom, I did not know you could be so compassionate." It was all due to the new person I was in Christ.

My journey with Christ instilled in me a desire to be a godly woman. As a part of my spiritual transformation after salvation, He led me to observe and interact with godly women through my church and Bible study. They taught me that I could be content with who I was — my gender, my roles and how God was shaping me. This was not a comfortable, overnight transformation; the process began more than thirty years ago and at times, my skin felt like it was gradually being peeled away to expose the damage before the healing could take place. Yet, the work of the Lord restores and rebuilds, making us *"oaks of righteousness"* for His glory (Isaiah 61:1-3, Italics mine). I saw that glory in the many Christian women God brought into my life, those women whose internal beauty and godly wisdom permeated my heart, mind and soul.

Not only did these godly women offer love and grace, they offered their prayers as well. When my husband, now a new believer, became hospitalized for the last time from another heart attack, Donna and the other women were our prayer warriors.

When tragedy occurs in our lives, it is the prayer warriors who call on our Heavenly Father asking for His strength and grace that upholds us. I knew this was the case when the following scene took place:

I watched God in His tender grace allow my husband a short respite so he would finish his last journey well. Gordy experienced an acute myocardial infarction, and he spent his last four and a half days in our local hospital. Unfortunately, during that time none of the pain medication had any affect on him; yet in spite of the excruciating pain, he exhibited Christ-like character. However, just a few hours prior to his death, his nurse tried another shot, and for the first time in four days, he rested — for about twenty minutes. He aroused with a slight jolt from the nap asking, "God — why?" I do not know what

God replied, but I know He did. For when he opened his eyes, he was starring into the face of Daneen, our middle daughter. Gordon smiled as if he had received his answer. Shortly after this event, at almost midnight, cradled in my arms, he went home to be with the Lord, a new creation in Christ.

When the monitors went off, the hospital staff rushed in and ushered me out. Upon leaving his room, my body became numb and tingly. I began to hyperventilate. The nurse took me to the waiting room while they attempted to resuscitate Gordy. The nurse sat me down on a couch in the waiting room and handed me a paper bag to breathe in. As my breathing returned to normal, a nurse came from Gordy's room and asked if I would like to go see him and say my final good-byes. Unfortunately, I took some ill advice from my sister-in-law, a recent widow whose experience in seeing her dead husband trauma-tized her. She tried to spare me the same experience.

I regret that choice even today. For unbeknownst to me, God had something special for us to see. My two younger daughters, Daneen and Susan, urged me to go with them, but I reluctantly shook my head no. My girls came back excited, saying, "Mom, Dad was smiling!" What a miracle the Lord had arranged for us! I had listened to a well-meaning person rather than that inner voice and my daughters' plea. Upon hearing my girls' news, it was as if God was saying to me, "Be at peace, he is home with Me."

Much transpired after Gordon's death financially, emotionally and spiritually as I grew in God's truth and grace. The shock and numbness of Gordy's death seemed to last for several weeks. It was as if I walked in a fog—numb and cold with no sense of real direction. As the shock wore off, other aspects of grief took over. I had seen and felt grief as a child, but soon realized I did not know how to handle bereavement in a healthy manner. I took to my Bible, reading how Jesus and God grieved. I learned to grieve from their example. The whole process took about three years, and it still visits me occasionally. One moment I was a wife; the next, a widow. Transition is never easy. Nevertheless, God, in His grace, led me on a new journey that has proven to be one I would not exchange for anything.

Looking back, two specific events still stand out for me. The first was about nine months into the grief process as I was on my way to work. I became extremely angry. I yelled, cursed and pounded on my steering wheel, "Why, God, why?" As I parked next to the river (where Gordy use to fish) to collect myself and seek forgiveness for the words I had said, the words of Christ came to me, *"Blessed are those who mourn, for they shall be comforted"* (Matthew 5:4, Italics mine). In that moment, I felt so consoled and calmed to know, really know, that God was with me and forgave me my loose, angry words.

The second impacting event was in regards to my finances and it reflected to me how Christ takes the responsibility and care of His children very person-ally. He used this event to build a deeper trust in Him and His care, protection and provision for me, His child.

I worked at an in-store bakery and earned about thirty-five dollars a week. This one week, I only had five dollars left for the rest of the week in my apron pocket. When it was time for me to go home, I reached into my pocket and my heart sank to my stomach — the money was gone. Panicking, I searched every trash can, swept the floor again just in case I missed the money the first time, and even dove into the dumpster in the back alley, all to no avail. Heartsick and panicked, I drove home heavily burdened. I did not want to upset my two girls, so upon arriving at home, I retreated to the bathroom and drew myself a bath.

The difference between just reading and believing the Scriptures is that you act on them. As I sat in the water crying, my washcloth seemed to take on the shape of a lily as Matthew 6:25-33 came to mind. *"Why are you worried...? Observe how the lilies of the field grow...Do not worry then...for your heavenly Father knows what...you need...But seek first His kingdom and His righteousness..."* (Italics mine). It is amazing how the Holy Spirit will bring to our remembrance Scripture to encourage and convict us. I knew that Christ was my life; and I could trust that even in this situation, which appeared to be insurmountable, He would help.

The next day He answered my prayers through a customer just coming from church. She purchased her goodies and left, but then returned within a couple of minutes. Puzzled and thinking I probably gave her the wrong change, I greeted her. She said, "I don't know why, but the Lord told me to come back and give you this." She handed me a rolled up five dollar bill. Receiving this gift, as if it was from the hand of Christ, I went in the back of the shop, fell down to my knees and cried, feeling enveloped by His presence. What a gift! What a miracle!

I saw God's hand and His marvelous grace work on my behalf often during this time. Somehow, He provided the strength to walk through the grief with joy, even though I was a mess inside. God had graciously placed me in that BSF study at just the right time. He knew biblical truth and godly women would surround me — God-fearing women who prayed, comforted and gave their support as I stood on the threshold of a new way of life — widowhood. I was no longer a wife, but still a daughter, mother, grandmother and friend. Best of all, I was God's child — redeemed and brand new. I am still friends with many of those BSF women. They continued to pray me through college, post-graduate work, breast cancer, back surgery and a host of other circumstances that arose in my life journey. God used them in unique ways.

Two other women that come to mind are Inez and Nellie. Both ladies were widows (much older than I was) and were the Lord's Titus 2 examples for me to follow. They took me under their wings after Gordy died and assisted me in learning to walk, not only as a Christian, but also as a widow. They remind me of the Apostle Paul's message to the believers of the early church that they were to follow his example (Philippians 3:17) as he was following Jesus Christ's example. Coincidentally, Inez (a former Sunday school teacher) had my daughters in her class at church. Nellie was a poet. Nellie and I rode together to Bible Study Fellowship class. With every lesson, came a new poem. They poured from a heart touched by God. Nellie gave me some of them and they are treasured — a gift from her heart to mine.

Another precious sister in the Lord, Jean, possessed the gift of organization — a skill that I lacked. She also had an infectious sense of humor. I was in awe of this bright, well-educated and highly disciplined woman. She epitomized all I was not. I was unorganized and uneducated. My laugh was loud and I thought, obnoxious. Jean meticulously helped me organize my lecture notes for a church retreat. She helped them flow and have order. I can safely say that any organizational ability I have obtained is primarily due to Jean's patience and example. Before Christ, my uncouth manners and Attention Deficit Disorder tendencies were hard to overlook. Jean showed me grace and great encouragement.

If my participation in Bible Study Fellowship was God's elementary school, I was about to enter spiritual high school. God used two teaching leaders, Jane and Margaret, both college graduates and serving Christ. Their example ignited a longing within me to be better educated. The desire for a higher education began when I saw how confident and articulate they were. Assessing my shortcomings, I concluded that obtaining a college education and becoming both confident and articulate probably would not take place in my lifetime. Oh, me of little faith! Jane and Margaret's lives and hearts permeated my being by their presence and gracious involvement in my life. They repeatedly instilled in me the saying, "Nothing is impossible with Christ!"

Even with their encouragement that in Christ nothing is impossible, I am sure my announcement during our study of Genesis surprised them. I believed with all my heart that just as God called Abram to Ur, He was calling me to go to college. Not only did this calling leave me in shock, it also left family and friends in shock as well. I wrestled with this calling and followed His lead, just not right away.

It took three years of wrestling with my human fears, insecurity and dealing with my own limitations. Praise God that during this time He did not give up on me. What I discovered was that God is not limited; however, I limited Him due to my lack of trusting Him — completely.

After finally surrendering to Him, I moved forward on His call, although not all of my fears and insecurities had dissipated. I left my family, job, ministry and friends to enter Western Baptist College in Salem, Oregon. I can give you every reason to believe that, for me, college ought to have been out of the question. Nevertheless, God's grace and wisdom demolished all my excuses. I was fifty years old, a high school dropout with a learning disability, poor English skills and only a GED. My shortcomings did not hinder His plans. God uses our weaknesses and shortcomings to demonstrate His strength and power. God divinely placed me among wonderful women in the BSF groups that had prepared me academically for this terrifying change. I had learned how to study in those ten years at BSF, not to mention the training in self-discipline, structure, perseverance and constant dependence on Him and His Word. He sent me forth with this strong foundation.

I would be remiss if I did not include another pivotal woman named Eleanor. Eleanor is witty and fun. She loves the Lord and His Word and is always ready, willing and able to share it with you. Eleanor was another BSF teaching leader who taught the first working women's class in Tacoma, Washington. I served with her for about four years prior to coming to college.

When I needed prayer, she prayed. When I was down, scared or feeling insecure, she called or sent a note always pointing me to our Lord and His sufficiency. Eleanor not only believed in what God had called me to do, but also believed in me. She does calligraphy. When I was going through my master's program, she sent several Bible verses, which I had framed and now hang in my home. Eleanor always has a ready laugh and is exceedingly gracious. She showed great concern and care when I went through cancer. When she called to check in on me, just hearing her lilting voice would raise my spirit.

God used these women to love, encourage and even confront me when needed — a sign of true friendship. These women were prayer warriors who also became like moms, sisters and daughters to me. Best of all, we are friends for eternity.

God used many women to touch my life, but if I included them all, I would run out of paper. I narrowed the list down to a very few women whose permeating influence was placed strategically by God at special times and various seasons of my life. They shined His glory and were His hands and heart in my spiritual, emotional and physical needs. I benefited greatly from their ministry. I pray that these ladies have reaped a harvest for their investment, known or unknown, in my life. May God honor these women and continue to bless their lives as their permeating influence continues to impact those women who cross their path.

Who has God brought into your life for influence? Who are you influencing? Is it for His glory?

Joan — Uniquely Designed

Genesis 2:22; Romans 8:28-29; James 1:2

J oan is a recreated young woman who married a youth pastor this past summer. Her changed life demonstrates the power and grace of her Lord. In her story, Joan divulges years of turmoil, self-destructive behavior and a poor view of her value and worth. This was due in part to thinking that her identity was found in popularity through grades, sports and relationships. Her life, before Christ, sounds like a soap opera until the Master had uniquely rede-signed Joan. Walk along with Joan as she shares her transformation.

Joan was born into a Christian family who regu-larly attended church. She heard all the traditional Bible stories and memorized Bible verses during her involvement in AWANA ("Approved Workman Are Not Ashamed," as taken from II Timothy 2:15). She asked Jesus into her heart when she was four years old after talking with her mother. Joan knew Jesus loved her, and she certainly wanted eternal life just as Jesus promised. However, this was the extent of what it meant to her to be a Christian. Unfortunately, for Joan, this mentality stayed with her until her junior year in college.

Sadly, the influences of those in her church did not represent Christ well. In her words, the people at her parents' church were "snotty and fake to each other; they gossiped and backstabbed." For Joan, church was boring, and she made up any excuse that kept her from attending. Going to that church was so painful that Joan often faked an illness. Because Joan wanted nothing to do with her parents' church or its people, she pushed her parents farther and farther away as well.

Like so many other teens during their middle school years, Joan led two lives. These lives were as different as night and day. At home, Joan presented herself in such a way that she would have been every parent's dream child. She was popular, a straight "A" student who was involved in year round sports activities. Therefore, there was nothing for her parents to be concerned about. However, unknown to her family, at school another side of Joan emerged. She began to hang around kids whose behavior was neither accepted nor tolerated within the Christian way of life. These teens were often in trouble at school or with the law and were sexually promiscuous. Joan soon realized that as she refused to participate in their loose lifestyle and inappropriate behavior, her newly found friends became skeptical about including her into their circle. This action by her peers ignited a sense of insecurity, which then became a driving need for acceptance.

It was about this time that Joan noticed boys did not pay any attention to her — at least not as much as she wanted. She decided it was because she was overweight, which, of course, was not the case. Therefore, Joan believed the answer was for her to diet. If she lost weight, then boys would notice her. After all, this is the message she received from magazines and the media. For Joan, skinny meant pretty.

Unfortunately, she first began this new diet regime in the seventh grade. Then, when that seemed to go unnoticed, she started skipping breakfast too. Joan deceived her parents into thinking she had fixed and eaten her breakfast before they got up. Joan was on a slippery track heading towards anorexia. In the eighth grade, she began trying to skirt eating dinner. As one could imagine, her weight loss was very noticeable and caused her friends and parents to question her. Joan's lies to her parents were catching up with her.

Joan rapidly lost her physical strength due to her lack of nutrition. Her lies became a trap, as her mental strength began to weaken, much like her body. Unable to keep up the charade any longer, Joan finally broke down and agreed to go to counseling. At this point, the five foot four inch Joan only weighed eighty-four pounds.

As always, God had His design on Joan and used her sister as one of His tools. Joan and her sister attended a concert hosted by the church her sister attended (a Calvary Chapel affiliate). Those attending sang with joy and appeared to devour each word that was preached from the Scriptures. The contrast between her parents' church and this church was staggering. This church service was a celebration whereas her parents' church was like attending a funeral. As a result, Joan greatly enjoyed this different church experience.

As soon as her parents heard Joan liked this new church, they jumped at the opportunity to get her involved. Joan's mother decided to attend this church herself, and the two went together. As a result, Joan began to learn the Word of God. It seemed like the first time she could remember really learning what God's Word meant, but it was not enough to change her distorted thought processes and internal destructive drive.

Joan entered high school, still recovering from anorexia. Soon she became active in school sports programs. Unfortunately, even though Joan had a lot going for her — a new church, her striving to beat the anorexia — the inner need for popularity had not changed. She thought for sure that having a boyfriend would be the answer to her struggle for acceptance. This driving force led her to John, a new friend with a "bad boy" reputation. They became a couple, and Joan received the attention she craved — but it was a false sense of security and the wrong type of attention.

Her new boyfriend, John, had a temper. This resulted in him fighting at the drop of a hat. Because of his short fuse, he scared off all of Joan's other male friends. At one point, Joan found herself physically between John and an old friend to stop a fight John had started. Unfortunately, John's continuous use of hard-core drugs and alcohol exacerbated his poor character qualities. To support his growing habit, he used to steal at night. Joan recalled, "One morning when he came to school, high and confused, he tried to give me a gift he had stolen the evening before, remarking that he was trying to be romantic." She refused the gift and John erupted much like Mt. St. Helens had done in the 1980's.

John was abusive and controlling, often leaving bruises on Joan's arms. His reputation for picking her up and throwing her into the school lockers was well known. His rationale after this action was to make her "remember whose girlfriend she was." John became paranoid, probably due to the drugs, and thought Joan was cheating on him. He often followed her wherever she went and frequently called her home to check on her. Nevertheless, again we can see God's hand at work as the police arrested John for stealing and expelled him from high school. John moved to another city; but his friends, who had accepted Joan because of him, now took up his vendetta against her after he left town. They continued to intimidate Joan until they dropped out of school.

Unfortunately, Joan did not learn from this experience. Confusion reigned as she continued to live in two different worlds: the church and the world. She went to church every Sunday, listened intently to the sermon and took notes, but her heart was still divided between God and the world. Although the pastor taught and explained each passage carefully, verse by verse, and she drank in the information, Joan's lifestyle did not change. The teachings from the Bible had little effect on her personal life and her relationship with the Lord. For years, Joan believed she was a Christian, though following Christ was not a heart choice but more of a directive made by others in her life. For Joan, Christian living and biblical discernment had not become a reality.

Soon a new man entered Joan's life. He was a long distance runner, an excellent student and the student body president. He seemed perfect. They started to spend time together, and then they began to date. He was good medicine for this bruised and battered young woman. He showed her respect and kept her smiling. However, he was from a church system of which Joan had no knowledge. Not only was its practices and doctrine completely unfamiliar to her, they were incompatible with her faith.

Surprisingly, Joan's parents seemed to support the relationship basing it upon how he treated her. Joan and her new boyfriend dated for two years, and then he left for Belgium to serve a two-year mission required by his church. They corresponded for a year before the relationship ended. Joan discovered from the biblical teachings that they were not a good match due to their theological differences.

This left Joan floating from one relationship to another during her senior year of high school. At the end of her senior year, she dated a professing Christian boy who ended up being a "pathological liar." He lied about things that were unimportant, such as where he grew up, his supposed achievements in school and where his parents were. His lying bothered her enough that she ended the relationship. His mother, unhappy about the break-up, began calling and harassing Joan and her parents.

This last relationship caused Joan to question herself and wondered why she continually got involved with the wrong types of men. Then misfortune, from the world's perspective, happened to Joan. She seriously injured her knee during volleyball season. Joan had to undergo surgery and physical therapy. Joan hoped for a college athletic scholarship because of her volleyball abilities. However, the colleges that were interested in her before her injury soon lost all interest in pursuing her. What looked like tragedy was really the hand of her Designer at work.

One school in Oregon did not give up on Joan because of her injury, so Joan decided to attend Western Baptist College (WBC) in Salem, Oregon. This decision brought an added bonus: Joan loved

Salem where the college was located. Now, she was actually going to leave the desert and live in the town she loved. Another plus for Joan was that Salem was not far from friends who were entering the University of Oregon located in Eugene, Oregon. Joan said, "I knew that WBC was where I was supposed to be, not because I wanted to be there, but because that is where the Lord wanted me to be. My friends were far away and this school was full of 'happy-go-lucky' Christians. Joan did not feel like she had much in common with this "holy group". However, she was able to connect with some students at the school who seemed to be more like her, living a divided life. Just because one attends a Christian college does not always mean one is living the Christian life.

Much to Joan's surprise, she met the star basket-ball player, a handsome junior, and they started dating. Unfortunately, this new relationship led Joan to drinking and partying at her boyfriend's apartment with his friends. This also was the same scene when she visited her friends at the University of Oregon. Her grades plummeted. Even though Joan knew she was heading down a dark and winding path, she continued on the path of destruction.

Joan soon found herself in a strange triangle with the jealous new boyfriend and his best friend, who also liked Joan. Almost as quickly as the relationship began, it ended. Then she became romantically involved with the best friend. To add to this confusing mess, Joan discovered that her new roommate was also her new boyfriend's former girlfriend. The tension and atmosphere in Joan's dorm room was anything but friendly. Red flags regarding this new relationship began to wave, but Joan did not pay any attention. She believed that having someone close would be better than no one at all. She found herself in another abusive relationship, both physically and mentally. The new boyfriend controlled her every move, telling her what she could and could not do. The saddest part about this situation is that she thought so little of herself she tolerated his demands and the subsequent harsh treatment.

Summer came and Joan returned home to her parents. It took about a month away from the abusive relationship before she realized the relationship had to end. Joan's parents agreed. He continued to call Joan, making promises to change, but she ignored him. Again, God intervened on Joan's behalf, arranging for this young man to suddenly leave and attend another college in California.

Summer ended and Joan's sophomore year began as badly as her first year had ended. She still looked for new friends that would quench her inner unsettledness and make her feel secure. Joan still lacked internal peace and confidence. She partied for months and then hit the proverbial brick wall.

Finally, Joan decided that she needed to make a change to her way of life. Unbeknownst to anyone, for more than a month, Joan locked herself in her dorm room, coming out only for classes and then returning to her self-imposed, solitary confinement. As a result, Joan became depressed leading to her being broken before the Lord. Joan said, "God knew my heart and knew I wanted to change. I began to really read the Word and desired to understand and make it a part of my life."

The Lord led her to read the book of James. James 1:2-4 became her life verse: *"Consider it all joy, my brethren, when you encounter various trials, knowing that the testing of your faith produces endurance. And let endurance have its perfect result, that you may be perfect and complete, lacking in nothing"* (Italics mine). In this passage, God spoke to her heart and reassured her that even though she had left

73

Him, He had not left her. He was still waiting for her, designing her and growing her up in the faith.

The Lord further proved His faithfulness by leading her to a group of amazing committed girls who had a great, healthy influence on Joan. These students lived for the Lord, and their impact on Joan was one of love, care and constant encouragement to trust and hold tightly to their Lord. These were her sisters-in-Christ and, for the first time in many years, she truly began to find joy in the Lord.

She decided to take a break from dating. She wanted her only focus to be on the Lord and their relationship and she told Him so. Joan says, "This was a big test for me to not have a male friend since boys had been such an integral part of my life. Over time, the Lord comforted me and I, for the very first time in my life, was okay not dating."

Unfortunately, Joan was unaware that another test was building and quickly approaching her. Its impact would hit her with hurricane force, like when Hurricane Katrina hit the coastland. Its intent was meant for her destruction; however, the outcome of any storm in the life of God's children is meant for their good.

The school authorities were already aware of her former "friends" poor conduct and behavior. Like rats on a sinking ship, they wasted no time to implicate her as well. When the school authorities confronted Joan, she told the truth, regardless of the natural consequences of her lack of Christ-like conduct. Her testimony, along with the testimonies of the other students, resulted in the expulsion of nine students for breaking the school's alcohol policy. She was honest with the dismissal board about the previous partying and her current endeavors to clean up her act. She headed into spring break without knowing whether the school was going to allow her to finish her semester.

The light bulb finally came on. She now could clearly see that these acquaintances were not "friends" but rather cohorts involved in the same sin. As one may imagine, Joan realized that in one fell swoop she lost both those she had believed to be friends, and the possibility the authorities would expel her from school. This double whammy left Joan feeling numb, lost and alone.

However, God, unknown to Joan, was working behind the scenes in her life. Even though God was with her, like a good parent, He did not protect her from the natural consequences of her sinful behavior and choices. The administration reached an agreement which clouded her next school term. The college assigned someone to Joan to hold her accountable in her behavior. Joan's accountability was no longer a voluntary matter — the school made her accountability a mandatory arrangement. If Joan violated the agreements, it would mean automatic dismissal.

Joan was determined to make good on this arrangement. She did not want to ruin what she believed was her last chance. To her credit, Joan requested her accountability partner to be her roommate as added insurance to help her adhere to the changes required. Joan wanted to do well; but she knew if she was to succeed, it needed to be done in the Lord's strength, not her own. The Lord had laid out a path for her to follow. Would she stay on His path or go her own way again? God had begun a good work in Joan's heart, and she chose to follow His lead regardless of the cost. This time, she did not want to disappoint Him anymore.

Unlike Joan's two previous college years this junior year began with excitement. Joan's life was changing for the good. Because of her destructive past, God placed a concern for the well being of other young women in her heart. That concern led her to change her college major from business to women's ministry. Because of this change, Joan would need to carry twenty-one credit hours both terms. Nevertheless, Joan was determined to work hard, live right and graduate knowing she had God's hand upon her and His blessings.

Joan now began to serve at her church in both children's ministry and in the women's ministry area. Amy, the overseer of both ministry areas, had a great influence upon Joan. She asked Joan to shadow her as she worked, and this gave her a "bird's eye" view of ministry in action.

After seeing and experiencing ministry from its high points to its low points, God ignited an unquench-able passion for ministry in Joan's heart. Even though she did not think this passion could become a reality, at the nudging of others, Joan contacted Amy to see if she could start working with the high school girl's group. Her heart's desire was to come alongside and show them the reality of the Lord and His love for them. Joan wanted to help them avoid making poor choices and taking the wrong path. She accomplished this by sharing her story a story of wanting attention, love and a sense of belonging, but pursuing them in a destructive manner rather than choosing to know, trust and lean on Jesus. Joan instilled in these girls that, unlike the world and its schemes for pleasure, ONLY Christ can permanently offer all they need and want.

Joan was in her senior year and carrying twenty-one units plus her ministry at the church. After Joan assisted Amy for two months, Amy decided to step down from the high school ministry so she could focus exclusively on children's ministry. This left Joan and another girl to carry the full responsibility of the high school girls. Amy reassured Joan, who felt intimidated and not ready for such a big task at first. She reminded Joan that the Lord is in control and that she needed to let Him do His work through her. Joan agreed. The transition went smoothly, and with it a tighter bond began to exist between the girls and Joan.

Joan understood her purpose and finally realized what it meant to have a relationship with the Lord. She has been working with high school girls for a year now and the doors are opening for outreach to the high schools in the Portland Metro Area. Today, Joan exhibits God's new and unique design — no longer concerned about the external person, but rather the internal woman whose goal is to glorify God, not focus on self. The Master Designer molded her to be a special influence in the lives of many young women as she lovingly guides them to grow in the Master's image — all to His glory!

Joan's gratitude is overflowing to God. She readily acknowledges His greatness and ability to do anything. Looking back at her life, she now finds herself in a place she never believed possible. Her blessings have overflowed. She marvels at the Lord's goodness; especially that He saved her.

Joan quotes Isaiah 14:24, *"The Lord of hosts has sworn saying, 'Surely, just as I have intended so it has happened, and just as I have planned so it will stand..."'* (Italics mine). The Lord is now Joan's source of security and acceptance. What He says goes!

Joan, like so many young girls, attempted to find answers to her internal pain through various avenues of escape: appearance, boys, booze and unsavory, unhealthy relationships. Some of you may be able to relate to Joan and her struggle for worth, identity and security which you have found in either people or things. However, once she accepted that God was her Master Designer, life did not get any easier, but she gained strength, wisdom, discernment and the ability to make good choices and stand firm in her Lord and God. Now all the testing and trials make sense to

Joan as she continues to exhibit fruit and be filled with His joy. *"Joy is not the absence of suffering, but is the presence of the Lord"* (Italics mine). Joan has discovered this as truth — have you?

According to Psalm 139, the hand of God has uniquely designed you. Does this truth empower you, or do "things" get in the way of you fulfilling His purposes? Like Joan, have you looked or placed your need for acceptance, love, contentment or happiness on external qualities? Those externals might include your looks, your shape, intelligence, success, talents or acceptance into a group. Nevertheless, just like Joan, you too, can begin to see yourself through His eyes and find that special acceptance, love, purpose and meaning to your life. You are His workmanship whether you want to admit it or not. God is the Master Designer for *all* His works. You can rest knowing He will accomplish what He began. God desires that His creation be remolded into a new and better image —

the image of His Son, Jesus Christ. This is where Joan found her life and her purpose; as a result, she now is serving her Lord, her new ministry and husband.

What will you choose?

Laurie — Elective Surgery

Romans 8:29, 12:1-2; Ephesians 4:17-19

Laurie is a new believer and she is experiencing a form of elective surgery in her life. It is elective because she is choosing to yield herself to the transformation process of becoming like her Lord. Laurie's journey (elective surgery) as a young Christian woman and single mother has not been without its moments of hardship, anxiety and fear. Yet because of her commitment to her Lord, Laurie has discovered that despite the tough times, she experiences great joy. This joy comes by being in Christ, letting Christ perform the surgery and discovering that her new existence is glorious.

When considering Laurie, the words of Jesus come to mind: *"For this reason I say to you, her sins, which are many, have been forgiven — for she loved much; but he who is forgiven little, loves little"* (Luke 7:47, Italics mine).

She attended a Bible study at my home and showed her eagerness to know the Scriptures and her Lord better. She asked questions to help her understand and was vocal about how much her Lord meant to her. Laurie came from a background that did little to promote any sense of significance and worth, but found both in Christ.

When Laurie and her twin sister, Lois, were eight, their mother Beth committed suicide. She shot herself, point-blank in the face, and young Laurie was the one who found her. Laurie remembers little regarding this incident or any events prior to her mom's death. It would seem the traumatic moment erased her good memories as well as the bad.

Laurie's dad worked hard, and she dearly loved him. He handled his grief and the responsibility of fatherhood as best he could. When school was over for the year, the girls (Laurie and Lois) went to live with their grandparents. Apparently, unable to handle the grief of his wife and fully aware of his responsibility as a father, he remarried within a year hoping to give the girls a substitute mother. He was unaware that his major purpose for marrying would never materialize because the girls and the new wife became bitter enemies. Their relationship lacked the love and respect needed so desperately by the twins.

The stepmother seemed to pick on Laurie the most. When Laurie put on a lot of weight, her stepmother used it as another way to torment her at home. Even at school, Laurie was unable to escape the taunting and the teasing. Her classmates scathing and harsh name calling added to the already boiling caldron of poisonous words that came from her stepmother. Unfortunately, this caused Laurie to develop a deep insecurity and sense of fear which left in its wake destruction, and a very unhappy childhood.

The struggle between Laurie and her stepmother continued. To add to their anger, the girl's stepmother sold their mother's belongings. Laurie believed she did this knowing how much she cherished her mother's things. The girls saw this act as one of retaliation, primarily focused towards Laurie as her criticism of Laurie seemed never ending. The angst towards her stepmom escalated. More resentment, hurt and anger developed when the girls discovered that their mother's social security check (intended for their care) was spent inappropriately.

Laurie's father worked in a job that required him to spend much time away from home. One day, he came home to an altercation between Laurie and his wife. She had accused Laurie of something she had not done. To get away from her, Laurie attempted to go upstairs but her stepmother grabbed hold of her leg, pulling her down the stairs. Both the stepmother and Laurie gave their own explanations, but Laurie found herself again in trouble. Laurie's stepmother appeared jealous of the relationship between her and her father. She was so jealous that if Laurie spoke to her father the stepmother demanded to know everything that was being discussed. Her father sensed trouble and asked Laurie to call him at work when she wanted to talk; Laurie complied. She did not want him to suffer anymore because of her relationship with his second wife. This made things difficult for Laurie, to say the least.

During high school, Laurie had a tonsillectomy and her parents administered an over-the-counter pain reliever. However, after taking it she began to feel strange. Her throat began to swell. She became scared. Laurie knocked on her parent's bedroom door to tell her stepmother how sick she felt. Her stepmother sent her to lie down on the couch. Laurie began to have difficulty breathing. With feelings of apprehension, Laurie walked gingerly up the stairs and knocked on the parent's bedroom door again. This time, her father got up and took her to the hospital. Laurie experienced an allergic reaction to the pain medication; had her father failed to get medical attention she could have died.

All this time, Laurie and Lois could see the grief their father carried for his first wife. He loved music and as he listened to old records and drank — both her dad and step-mom were alcoholics — his mind and heart were on Beth, who was gone. He felt guilty about the situation in which he had placed the girls; he loved them and they loved him. The sisters tried to protect him because he was in such deep emotional pain. Consequently, they made few demands for his love and acceptance.

Due to this void in their life, the girls sought love and acceptance elsewhere. They first tried attending several churches, even a youth group, but the family gave them no encouragement to continue. The girls felt emptier than before and saw no need to look to church to fill their void. No one in her family knew Christ, and no one sought after Him. Is it any wonder that at thirteen and fourteen years old Laurie began a long affair with drugs? It started with infrequent use and then escalated. She began to include alcohol and cigarettes into the mix as well. This behavior then led to boyfriends, and that eventually led to a pregnancy. News of the pregnancy crushed Laurie's father.

Although pregnant, Laurie decided to continue her schooling, a rarity in her small town. After her son was born, Laurie and the child's father moved out of state. However, Laurie soon missed her twin sister, so they returned home. Laurie's marriage became difficult, and they separated. Laurie desired to finish her education. She looked into the teen mother school; but it did not appeal to her, so she returned to her former high school. The school informed her that she could return and graduate but it would not be with her own class. She was disappointed about this decision, but was determined to pursue and finish her education.

God used all these circumstances in Laurie's life, and some special people to get her attention. One such person was a kindhearted woman who helped her find daycare for her son. A Christian, this child-care giver watched Laurie's child free of charge. With the help of that "wonderful woman," Laurie was able to attend and graduate from high school.

After graduation, Laurie continued to work at a fast food place and became a night manager, her drug use escalating. She had an affair with a married man — her best friend's husband, no less. Eventually, the friendship and the relationship with the man ended.

Both sisters were desperate to move to a better part of town. An older sister, who they had had little contact with, came forward and agreed to rent them a place. The move came at the right time and things seemed to go well. Suddenly, their sister decided to evict them with only one month's notice. Rather than wait the month, Laurie and her sister overreacted and moved out immediately.

Lois had recently introduced Laurie to, what she believed was a nice man. So when this new predicament surfaced, Laurie made another rash decision. She moved in with this new boyfriend and his buddy.

Laurie had limited visitation rights for her son to come and visit. So when Laurie's son would come to visit a battle ensued between her and the new boyfriend. However, when the boy's father discovered that her life was full of chaos and drugs he sought full custody of the boy and won. Laurie was shattered. Shortly after this event, the boyfriend accused Laurie of being involved with his roommate. His accusation was unfounded and not true. This incident raised her awareness and she began to see signs that her boyfriend was not only extremely jealous, but also paranoid. This resulted in the relationship ending.

Now that Laurie no longer had her son full time, her life began spiraling downward. She began selling drugs. She lived with relatives for a while until meeting a woman who was willing to rent her a room. Soon after moving in, the woman and her friend broke into Laurie's room. Laurie left. The property owner later accused Laurie of running up her phone bill plus owing her money. Laurie's anger reached the boiling point, and she returned to get her things. The woman called the police, who arrested Laurie, but released her soon after. It took a long time, but Laurie finally retrieved her belongings. She also discovered that her stepmother had bought some of her things from the property owner and would not return them to Laurie.

As Laurie and her sister continued on their destructive course, she found out some surprising news — her biological mother had a son prior to marrying her father and had put him up for adoption. A nationally syndicated television show contacted the girls with this news, attempting to put the families in touch with each other. Laurie and Lois flew back east, taped the show and then returned home.

They had very little time together with their newly found brother, but decided to have a family reunion so the rest of the family could meet him. Laurie's summer was very busy with the reunion, then a trip to Montana for a friend's wedding. Laurie decided to stop using drugs temporarily for her trip. But without them to stimulate her body, Laurie had nothing to help keep her awake.

Shortly after returning home from the wedding and still in a somewhat weakened state, her son asked her to call his grandma, her stepmother, who lived in a little red house. She ignored his request, so he called her. While speaking with his grandma, she asked to speak to Laurie and told her that her dad had an accident at work. In shock and fear, Laurie immediately got on a bus for the sixteen-hour trip. When she arrived, her twin did not meet her as had been previously arranged. Instead, her cousin met her and informed her that her father was dead. Upon hearing the news, Laurie collapsed.

Later that year, Laurie began experiencing "charley horses" behind her knees and her hands began cramping. The cramps moved to her chest, and she began to experience breathing problems. An emergency room physician diagnosed her with Rhybdomyalisis, a common disease among the elderly. Laurie's muscles were breaking down and her kidneys would eventually begin to fail.

During her three-day hospitalization, Laurie's doctor told her that if she continued using drugs, she would die. She stopped using drugs and gained fifty pounds. During her recovery, Laurie lived with her sister. She began dating again and ended up pregnant. This pregnancy was a blessing, and the baby she was carrying gave her a vital reason to get off and stay off drugs permanently. She had a reason greater than herself — her unborn baby.

Laurie's living arrangement with her sister was stressful because her twin still used drugs. One day, tempers flared between the two sisters. Pregnant Laurie and her son had to leave, but had no place to go. Thankfully, her stepmother put her up in a hotel. Shortly after arriving at the hotel, her son returned to his father.

A month before her baby was due, Laurie visited friends and began to feel ill. She went back to the hotel where her water broke. No one was there to help her, so she got herself to the hospital. She was alone and experiencing a tough labor. An "awesome nurse" kept an eye on her even after her shift had ended. Laurie gave birth to a little baby girl.

Laurie became motivated to change and utilized community resources for housing and on-the-job training programs. She worked for a state agency and later an insurance company. She was finally on the road to recovery. Laurie began to dream of better things ahead — she longed for a car to replace the one she feared was going to break down, a real home where she didn't have to worry about drug-using neighbors and a safe neighborhood and environment for her daughter and son to live in when he visited. As Laurie was intent on making positive changes in her life, she thought about her aunt and uncle.

Laurie had a great love and affection for her aunt and uncle. The sisters came to know them when the girls lived with the grandparents during the summer months. Her aunt and uncle were in love with Jesus. They had a great testimony with all the family members. Laurie recalled that her aunt had a glow about her. She always seemed at ease and relaxed, as if someone else was bearing the weight of her burdens. Laurie remembers that at her father's funeral she needed a dress. Both the aunt and the uncle, hearing of this need, took her shopping for a dress even though they were mourning. Somehow, her uncle managed to make this moment better.

Laurie loved and appreciated her aunt and uncle and saw a lot of power behind her aunt's prayers. Once, when one of her cousins called, he expressed his own concern about his financial situation because some of his customers were behind in their payments. Laurie's aunt prayed with him at that very moment, over the phone, and the next day he received money owed him from his customers — not just one, but at least five of his customers. Laurie expressed a desire to experience the kind of relationship they had with their Savior who was so full of grace and mercy. She had seen His power demonstrated through their prayer for her cousin.

Before Laurie could inquire further about the aunt and uncle's faith, they died in a car accident caused by a drunken driver. At their funeral, the pastor presented the Gospel and then gave an opportunity to the bereaved to stand if they wanted to accept Christ. Without hesitation, Laurie stood up and repeated the simple prayer for salvation.

When she returned home, she started attending a small church. However, because of her insecurities, she was scared to visit the bigger churches in her area. Laurie figured once she had some confidence, felt more comfortable and was not so biblically ignorant, she would attend a larger church.

Subtle changes started to take place. Transformation was happening. Even her fourteen year old son said one day, "Mom, you've changed." The change may have been unsettling for him, but she knew it was for the better.

Laurie's daughter loved to sing, and Laurie became convicted by the Holy Spirit about her music choices. When her daughter was in the car, Laurie only played a Christian radio station. She did not want her girl to hear and repeat any of the lyrics that came from the music she liked. Then when her daughter was out of the car, she would change the station back to her music. As time went on, Laurie became more and more uncomfortable and offended by her choice of music. She decided to join her daughter in listening only to Christian radio.

The Lord has done wonderful things for Laurie in a short amount of time in her life. Do you recall her dreams about a house, job and car? Well, she has realized all the longings of her heart. She has a car — and not just any car — the one she really wanted. She has a house. In addition, she is working in a law office for Christian attorneys. The Lord has blessed her abundantly and she is growing in the Word, attends church regularly and has just signed up to help in the children's ministry area. In addition, she has a new Christian husband and a baby on the way.

Laurie says, "I never knew that there was such a love like the Lord's — and forgiveness. Who else do you know that you can ask forgiveness from and who willingly forgives you and then forgets about it? Parents should love their children unconditionally as the Father above does. Even though I am new in my faith, the Lord has certainly shown me what He is capable of."

Going from salvation to the transformation process has not been easy, but it is fulfilling. Laurie is learning that to be joyful, she needs to yield her life to the Lord on a daily basis. Since she is no longer her own — she was bought with a high price — Christ's life.

Through her life Laurie had experienced character flaws which were harmful and led her to make wrong choices. Sometimes they were due to a cut to the heart from a trusted friend or a blow to the head from an enemy. However, Laurie is learning that God is better than any earthly friend, but there is a cost. One does not need to fear the transformation to become like His Son. The surgery He performs may hurt momentarily, but the eternal reward is immeasurable. Laurie entered this process willingly. She is learning the benefits of undergoing His transforming surgery.

By yielding your life to the Lord and undergoing His elective surgery you, too will experience the same joy Laurie enjoys each day.

God's children need not dread the Great Physician or His type of surgery which produces character change. In order for this type of change to transpire, however, each believer must yield to the Surgeon's Hand. The outcome of God's corrective surgery is always successful (unlike most plastic surgery). After all, He is the Great Physician and His work lasts for eternity.

Won't you be like Laurie and seek to see yourself through His eyes? He created you in the womb of your mother and knew who you were to become.

It stands to reason then, He is the ONLY one who can bring His purpose to pass. Like Paul the Apostle, you too can say: *"I have been crucified with Christ; and it is no longer I who live, but Christ who lives in me; and the life which I now live in the flesh I live by faith in the Son of God, who loved me, and delivered Himself up for me"* (Galatians 2:20, Italics mine). Perhaps you can paraphrase Paul's words in this way: "I only have one life to live. May it always be for His glory and honor."

Romans 12:1-2 tells us to offer our *"...bodies a living and holy sacrifice, acceptable to God, which is [our] spiritual service of worship..."* and to be *"... transformed by the renewing of your mind, that you may prove what the will of God is, that which is good and acceptable and perfect"* (Italics mine). When we present our bodies to the Lord without restraint, it is much like signing up for elective surgery. Unlike a physical operation, God's spiritual surgery changes us internally and shapes us more and more into the image of Christ, which ultimately affects our outward appearance.

Are you open to being changed by His surgery?

Marie — The Reality Factor

Isaiah 42:7; Acts 10:40-41;
Ephesians 5:11-17

Marie is a friend who was raised in a home committed to Roman Catholicism. The church was their reality. Unfortunately, for Marie, this reality created much confusion and doubt as the religious system led to a form of bondage built on fear. It kept Marie tied in knots through all eight years of grade school as she studied under the scrutiny of nuns and priests. Besides that pressure, she also had to contend with their extremely high standard of discipline, which seemed almost unattainable.

As Marie grew up, her reality was based on the Roman church's doctrine, along with its rituals and traditions. Her fear took on a life of its own. She was told many times if she disobeyed the church, she was destined to hell.

Marie's story involves her struggles as she journeyed to find freedom from her fear that hell would be her eternal destination. She eventually found that freedom and much more; she found eternal security, love, forgiveness and acceptance through her relationship with Jesus Christ. The church dogma and rituals were replaced with God's absolute truth and a joy found in the one and only true reality of God's Word and His Son, Jesus Christ.

Marie states, "I was born into a family of generational belief and commitment to the Roman church." Through her parents' strictness and staunch belief in the church, she was heavily indoctrinated into the "truth" of this one religion. In hindsight, Marie can see the indoctrination done by both her parents and the church was a form of brainwashing, but she also could see the sovereign hand of God. Even as a young child, God had placed an awareness of Jesus in Marie's heart and a deep longing to know Him.

Growing up, Marie's religious and spiritual experiences were plagued with confusion, fear and often pain. Her perception of God was not based on the reality shown in the Bible. "How could He love me, and who was I to think that He would even know I existed? After all, He was nothing more than that 'powerful big being' that was waiting to catch me doing what He considered wrong so I would suffer great punishment." These thoughts shaped her perception of her own significance and value as a person. She saw herself as one who was in constant sin and unable to do anything right. The harder she worked at being an obedient, respectful and caring daughter and sister, the more she felt she had failed and fallen short. "I was, in essence, steeped in darkness."

Around the age of nine or ten, Marie began to feel within her a deep longing and loneliness. She turned to prayer. Even though Marie was raised in an environment based upon repetitious prayer, now her prayers took on a new form — one of a simple conversation with Jesus. She had heard vaguely about Jesus, but in "sketchy" ways and questioned if He even existed. However, if He did, Marie knew she wanted Him to be her friend, even though she was unsure what that meant.

Based on her previous training, Marie was destined for hell and therefore, believed there was no way she would be invited to heaven. A constant theme ran through her mind: "He doesn't even know I exist." As she grew into her twenty's, Marie felt she had little to no significance or value. She says,

"I saw myself as a dull pebble on the beach of more shining, brilliant and beautiful pebbles. Certainly He would only see the other pebbles — not me, for I am obscure and buried beneath those more noticeable ones as long as I live."

To add to this ominous fear, her mother took Marie to a "mission" one evening to hear from a visiting priest who spoke to the parishioners regarding their duties as good, practicing church members. In a voice that sounded like thunder he said, "Anyone who leaves this church will be condemned forever to the fires of hell." Marie recalls telling her mother that the priest was wrong; she knew other people that did not attend her church and had heard them talk about the relationship they had with a very wonderful and loving God.

As she reflected on this incident, Marie saw God's hand at work that evening and knew it was a turning point in her life. Her quest for truth began at twenty-four years of age, an odyssey to seek Him out, to know Him in a personal way. She even had a faint glimmer of hope that perhaps this desire was possible. *"Delight yourself in the Lord; and He will give you the desires of your heart"* (Psalm 37:4, Italics mine).

Marie realized that in life, "those things that are worthy and worthwhile do not happen overnight." Much preparation needed to take place within her heart and mind in order to receive and recognize "those things that are worthy and worthwhile." She knew nothing about the Word of God because her religious training insisted that only learned theologians were able to open the pages of the Bible. Doing otherwise would be committing a grave sin of disobedience.

Again Marie saw God's real hand at work. Small Bible study groups began to spring up, and she jumped at the opportunity to participate in one. The study proved somewhat disappointing because the approach was more oriented towards feelings rather than an in-depth study about what God could say to her personally. Yet in spite of her disappointment, she was able to realize some messages as she read through the Scriptures.

In the meantime, Marie was confronted by challenges as a wife and mother. She and her husband were both raised in families where the old adage, "children are to be seen and not heard" prevailed. Marie and her husband became like a "trash compactor;" their communication and interaction with one another compressed into one messy bundle. In addition to this, their own parents attempted to control and dominate their decisions regarding church, marriage and extended family. Marie's husband had grown up with little spiritual influence, much less training, to be a spiritual leader in the home. Marie kept trying to implement her religious practices and influences into their marriage but it was useless. "My husband obviously believed that going to church on Sundays was about the extent of what he could give and that it was sufficient." Still, Marie could see God's hand protecting them from false doctrine and preparing them for a real relationship with Him.

In Matthew 11:28-30, Jesus says, *"Come to Me, all who are weary and heavy-laden, and I will give you rest. Take My yoke upon you and learn from Me, for I am gentle and humble in heart, and You shall find rest for your souls. For My yoke is easy and My burden is light"* (Italics mine). Some theologians have said that these verses are like a self-portrait; this is the only place in Scripture whereby Christ tells us what He is like. These words were so meaningful to Marie that she placed them on a magnet on her refrigerator. Marie clung to them with tenacity because they held great promise that this God, who she had begun to believe in, would accept her and love her just as she was.

Her marriage was not without its issues. Poor communication between Marie and her husband led Marie to believe she no longer loved him. Thoughts of divorce began to enter into her mind but she knew that her children, two toddlers, had to be considered. Marie had also been taught that divorce was a grave sin, and she did not want to displease the God she was seeking as a friend. The wrestling in Marie's soul left her tortured and miserable.

One morning, Marie's husband completely ignored her as he left for work — no kiss goodbye, no "have a good day" — nothing. She was broken and crying. Marie began to tell God that she could not live this way anymore. Then a thought formed in her mind: "Why would you want to allow Satan to destroy something that someday could be very beautiful for God?"

Words flowed from Marie's heart and out of her mouth to her God. "Lord God, look what I've done with my life, with our marriage — look at the mess I've made of things. Please forgive me. Lord, I want to know You in a personal way — please come into my heart from today forward and be my friend. Show me Your ways and lead me in the way that I should go. Help me trust you." At that point in her life, Marie knew nothing about the salvation message, the sinner's prayer or about having a personal relationship with Christ. She only knew of her deep need and desire to change. "I wanted to have a deeper belief in Him and become what He wanted me to be," Marie says. "I wanted to break free of the prison of doubt, confusion, depression, anger, destruction and darkness that I had been in bondage to for so long."

Once Marie surrendered to the Great Living God of the Universe, she began to see miracle after miracle happen in her life. Some may consider these just small happenings, but not this woman. Marie's spirit soared; her heart skipped with joy and thoughts regarding this wonderful God who heard her cry became intimately involved in repairing the broken pieces of her life. He healed Marie's marriage and filled her with thanksgiving and praise.

Marie's struggle and battle between her parents and the church continued. She believed she needed to stay loyal to the church so as not to hurt her parents. For the next seventeen years, Marie and her husband remained in the family's religion. They both struggled with a loss of victory over sin in their lives and concern about raising their children with godly principles, even though they were not sure what those principles should be at this point. Spiritual progress was like one step forward and two steps back much of the time. Their discontentment grew.

One of the blessings that surfaced for Marie and her husband was open communication as they talked about their options in finding a church. "My husband would tell me we could leave any time and we need not fear condemnation or rejection," she recalls.

Even though she feared leaving the church, she witnessed the hypocrisy and the double standards being lived out in what some thought to be "spiritual" families. The fruit of this dark religious structure could no longer be ignored. Marie watched the church change its laws, decrees and stories that had placed great horror and fear in her heart as a child. One such story was that if a baby died they would never see Jesus, but go to a place called "limbo" for eternity. "As an adult, I saw these stories as scare tactics. These were ways used to keep me in fear so that I would never leave." However, in her time of fear and indecision, one particular Bible story stood out.

As Marie read the Bible on her own, Matthew 13:3-9 caught her attention. It was the parable of the soils and tells of a farmer who scatters seeds in four different soils. The first was the hard soil by the roadside where, when seeds were tossed, birds came and devoured them. The second soil was rocky, and the seeds could not find deep enough soil to take root. The third soil was thorny and when the seed sprouted, the thorns grew and choked them out. The fourth soil was soft and fertile, the seeds sprouted and flourished, yielding a great harvest. Marie says the Holy Spirit used this story to direct her mind and heart toward the Gospel.

Marie's eyes were opened and could see that though the Bible was used in her now former religion, it was disconnected from a personal relationship with Christ. The church's teachings were based on a three year liturgical cycle, taken from the New Testament epistles and the gospels of Matthew, Mark, Luke and John.

"Never before had the Word spoken to me," she says, "but I knew that I wanted my life to be like the fertile soil — it needed to reflect Christ and His love. I wanted to be His completely."

Through the course of many years and many events, Marie's husband began a long commute to a new workplace in another city. They concluded that they needed to move closer, so they prayed. They did not know if this was the Lord's will but decided to put the house up for sale and see what happened. It sold within ten days. They also decided that when they moved, they would pull out of the Roman Catholic Church. This answered their prayer of twenty years.

Marie had also been praying for ten years that God would lead them to a "rag-tag" group of Christians — who first of all loved the Lord with all their hearts, loved His Word and truly loved one another. Before they moved, Marie became friends with Karen, a woman from her work. They started commuting together. "I noticed Karen was different than others and discovered she was a Christian. She displayed joy, faith, hope — she was truly one who allowed Christ to shine through her." Marie asked her about her church and if she thought they could come sometime. Karen responded right away with, "Well, how about this Sunday?"

Marie was stunned with her answer. "We had planned to church shop for a year and step aside from organized religion due to our experience with the Roman church. It all appeared so evil. We only wanted to follow Christ and come to know Him more deeply and intimately."

That Sunday morning in 1989, Karen and her family were out of town, but Marie and her husband decided to be brave. They were serious and committed to seeking Christ in their lives. "We were shocked as people greeted us in the parking lot and greeted us at the door. They sang wonderful songs of worship and praise. They acted as if they really loved one another and it was evident that they loved the Lord. The true Word of God was preached, and I cried throughout the service and for several weeks afterwards. I knew, without a shadow of a doubt, that God had answered my prayers. He had led us home. He had brought us to a place we could be bathed in His Word. We were committed and resolved to follow Him regardless of the cost, and we have been blessed beyond measure."

Marie's life has been a process of change and growth as God continues to shape her and reassure her of His love for her. "My humble prayer is that the Lord will never allow me to lose sight of that dark place, full of despair, which He brought me out of many years ago. Little did I know as a small child, a young girl and even a woman that this wonderful Lord and Savior wanted *me* to be His. I desire to live my life with a thankful heart for all He has done, and to live my life in such a way as to bring Him the honor and glory due Him."

"The reality of His longing for me and His desire that I trust Him, lean and depend on Him may be hard for some to comprehend, but it is the truth, and that truth was personified through Jesus Christ's birth, death and resurrection. This is true reality — for Christ is truth." Jesus said, "*I am the way, and the truth, and the life; no one comes to the Father but through me*" (John 14:6, Italics mine).

There are many forms of reality. Many believe in a reality that is generalized from their life experiences, mental illnesses (like schizophrenia and other delusional disorders), false religions based on fear, guilt and shame or some form of selfish love. For Marie, reality was based upon her being raised in a belief system requiring total commitment to a church, rather than Jesus Christ.

No matter what your background, believe that God will answer those who truly seek Him. This, dear reader, is the reality factor. In what, or who, is your reality based? Is it based on a church, denomination or your personal relationship with God's Son, Jesus Christ?

Dawn – A Transformed Vessel

Isaiah 61:1-3; Ephesians 4:23-24;
Colossians 3:5-10

Her story brings honor to the Lord as she has submitted to God's hand while He works to transform and bring victory in her life. Dawn is a wonderful and remarkable woman. She serves in a camp ministry with her husband, Dave, at Mt. Gilead in Northern California. As I came to know, respect and admire Dawn for what God allowed her to overcome, and the women who had been such a special influence in her life, I knew her story needed to be included.

God is so creative in the way He calls and speaks to us individually. At times we may laugh at the way He brings about His purposes in the lives of His chosen. In Dawn's case the Lord used the transformation of her neighborhood to change her life forever. Now sit back and read in awe and wonder as her story unfolds.

Dawn, like so many early in life, attended Sunday school, learned the Ten Commandments and Bible stories, but that is where her spiritual training ended. Her Sunday school teacher appeared to lack a personal, life-changing knowledge of Christ, and although she taught her lessons well, she did not pass on the gospel or a real awareness of God's transforming power. It demonstrated more "head knowledge" rather than "heart knowledge." But the Lord has promised that when we truly search for Him we will find Him. Dawn discovered the truth when the Lord brought a special lady into her life. He would use her influence to reach Dawn who earnestly was seeking Him.

During Dawn's junior high years, the wild property across the street from where she lived made way for three new homes. This displeased Dawn because she loved the outdoors — all of nature — and the plot of land which was her special private sanctuary. But God knew what He was about to accomplish in her life and set His divine plan and purpose into motion.

One of God's own, Sharon, moved into one of those new homes. As time progressed, Dawn and Sharon developed a relationship that has now spanned over thirty years and is still going strong.

Sharon had children Dawn's age and was full of fun. Over the course of time, Dawn was intrigued by her sense of purpose; she always seemed to know where she was going.

Around the time of this budding relationship, another development transpired that gripped Dawn's mind and heart. Her Uncle Mike was diagnosed with terminal cancer. Haunted by thoughts of his impending death, Dawn suddenly recognized the fragility of human life. Her quest for answers about God took on a frantic state.

Her deep soul searching made her more attentive in church. As she began to attend Sharon's church, what she heard started to make sense. Dawn was hearing the true gospel message unlike the teachings of her previous church. God had a plan for her life. She was a hopelessly lost sinner in need of a gracious Savior. It was at this time that the Holy Spirit took the blinders off her eyes. She now knew that she must confess Christ as the Son of God before men and confess her love for God to others. However, much like her old church, Dawn's belief was intellectual rather than experiential, head knowledge versus a heart change.

Although Dawn had fun as a teenager her unsettled soul was on a serious quest for spiritual answers. Recognizing Dawn's need, Sharon invited her to hear a visiting evangelist, Sammy Tippit.

The evangelist shared about a holy and righteous God and how even our best efforts are not enough to get us into heaven. He then shared Romans 3:23-24, which tells us that all have fallen short of God's glory. He shared that Jesus paid the penalty for all our sin. Mr. Tippit further explained that through belief in Jesus Christ and accepting His gift of salvation, comes the cleansing and forgiveness from our sins. Dawn desired salvation and made that commitment by going forward to solidify her pledge. When asked why she came forward to receive Christ she answered, "Because I love Jesus." An elder spoke with her and led her in a prayer of confession and commitment. Dawn truly believed that the moment she said the words "I love Jesus," she became a transformed individual. Acts 16:31 states, *"Believe in the Lord Jesus, and you will be saved... "* (Italics mine). This type of belief in this statement is a belief of the heart, not the head. Dawn acknowledged this to the elder and now is a new creation in Christ. Now He would lead her life, goals, dreams and she would know His peace.

Like many, Dawn's life turned upside down after accepting Christ. She vividly remembers the first day back at school, wondering many times if God would be pleased with her actions. Dawn experienced a whole new awareness of sin. A huge sense of peace and joy was evident in her being. She began using Scripture to filter her choices in music and language. As the Bible convicted her on these issues, she obeyed. Her faith grew tremendously and so did her desire to know the Word of God. She attended church every possible chance she got. Sharon took her under her wing as the Titus passage tells older women to do. Dawn was led through a Navigators Bible study and the Book of John during the discipling process.

In the midst of all her spiritual growth, Dawn's life took an unexpected turn. At eighteen years old, she experienced her first panic attack. She was driving on the freeway in Seattle with Sharon and began to feel dizzy; her heart was beating relentlessly fast and hard. Thinking she might pass out, Dawn pulled over and had Sharon drive the rest of the way. It was the beginning of a twenty-five year disability over which she had no control.

Her sister, Sue, also struggled with panic attacks, but Dawn thought she should be immune to them. After all, she diligently memorized Scriptures and taught Sunday school. How could *she* have the same affliction as her sister? How could she be victimized by such a cruel and debilitating disorder? Dawn had to make many changes to avoid having an attack. She sometimes had to leave a classroom unexpectedly, drive out of her way to avoid a bridge or make every kind of excuse she could to avoid flying in an airplane. Dawn felt humiliated. She battled with the misconception that being a victorious Christian meant she would not suffer emotional or psychological trials and disorders. Dawn also mistakenly believed that memorizing and quoting Scripture verses would free her from her prison of fear.

During Dawn's college years, her on-going panic attacks and job as a crisis counselor with troubled girls left her disillusioned. She found she was unable to rescue the troubled teens, and even though her heart ached for them, she was also afraid of them. Dawn was preparing for a degree in psychology and dreamed of working with abused or neglected youth.

She wanted to be able to counsel them, but doubted her abilities.

She recalls asking, "What's wrong with me, God? What is it? Why can't I just counsel and deal with their issues and discipline them when they need it?" She was twenty-two years old and wanted to rescue these girls but couldn't. She left that job after just three weeks — wiser, yet absolutely broken because she thought she had failed God and the girls. Shortly afterwards, she took a job that involved no emotional ties and little stress. It allowed her more freedom to come and go from work with little responsibility.

Now at the age of forty-three, Dawn looks back on that time and sees that her heart was burdened because of those troubled girls but had misinterpreted this as God's calling on her life. She learned that a burden does not always equate to His calling. Dawn was led by her heartache and mistakenly believed she could fix the girls and their families. This experience left Dawn feeling guilty and defeated. Sometimes at our lowest point, when we finally come to the end of ourselves, God steps in and points us in a new direction.

For God had prepared a new ministry for Dawn via her new husband, Dave. Dave had been called to be a Program Director at a local Seattle camp. Dave and Dawn were opposites. He was gifted, confident in his skills and recognized his great worth and strength in Christ. Conversely, Dawn had virtually lost any sense of value between her panic and the failure to succeed at working with people.

For someone struggling with panic attacks and self-esteem, comfort and familiarity are paramount. They provide stability for a person desperately wanting to feel safe. This need became evident when Dave took another job eight hundred and fifty miles from home. "We packed and this became a very sad day for me. My mother, who usually does not cry, sobbed as we drove away. I would have unpacked in a moment if the opportunity had arisen, but God had a different plan. We knew in the core of our being that this was what God wanted for us. So off to Sebastopol, California we went." Dawn and her family were to serve in a camp ministry at Mt. Gilead.

"I did not jump into ministry but went to work in the billing office at a hospital," Dawn says. "This position required three things I did not enjoy: numbers, finances and being organized; but again God's tender mercy sent me a precious woman named Julie. Julie believed in me. She was twenty-five years old herself, but unlike me, she was confident and knew where she was going."

"I was struggling spiritually because of my panic attacks and did not know what to do with them. In a Bible study, I attempted to be transparent and although the women were gracious and kind, they had no idea how to help nor had they struggled to this extent.

When I left the study, I felt more ashamed and alone than ever. I confided in an older Christian woman, but felt judged as an unsuitable role model — and definitely not suitable for serving in ministry."

Needless to say, Dawn was crushed, not by what was said or left unsaid, but because of her own frail, insecure spirit. She began to build thick walls around her heart. Yet, even in this time of heavy discouragement, God provided a gleam of hope. Dave and Dawn became parents. "I loved being a mom and playing with my boys," she says.

"During this period, I faithfully read my Bible and prayed, for it was only the Lord that was holding my nerves together." Dawn began to attend a new Bible study closer to home. She had previously met the leader, Jan, a woman who appeared rock solid in her faith and in the knowledge of God's Word. Jan seemed to be the most compassionate person Dawn had ever met.

"Because of the Bible study, I saw Jan each week. I became convinced I could learn from her and invited her to my house," Dawn recalls. "It was awkward; I did not know how to make coffee and tea made me gag. However, Jan was gracious and kind. I never saw myself as the hostess type, and I believe that Satan was eager to thwart this encounter with Jan because it became the most significant key to being set free from my panic. As we talked, I unburdened my heart to her. I shared how I had memorized whole passages on God's peace to no avail. Jan encouraged me to continue attending the study that she taught. I guess I just wanted her to fix my problems... again, not God's plan for Jan."

"There was great wisdom in being in the Bible study, rather than Jan and I having a face-to-face meeting each week discussing issue after issue. People in need can suck the life out of others because we refuse to ponder God's truths and fellowship with *all* believers. There is value in counseling, but knowledge of God's truths and fellowship lays the foundation for effective counseling. This factor is critical to healing and wholeness and living the transformed life God intended for His children. Through this knowledge and accountability healing can happen quicker because it allows others, and the Lord, to reveal truths about ourselves that we cannot or will not see."

Dawn remained well grounded in God's Word, yet the wall she built to guard her heart stood firm. She continued to hide the depth of her fears from others, convinced that she would be judged or perceived as unstable. The times she did choose to share, she felt her insecurities reinforced. Only Dave and Jan made her feel safe.

God continued to stretch Dawn through two particular challenges. The first was when Dawn was asked to share her testimony on the power of discipleship to thirty women. "This request created two dilemmas:

first, I had to share publicly and second, [I had] to share something that stirs my soul so deeply. This approach-avoidance conflict I experienced is classic — one you can find in Old Testament characters like Abraham, Moses and David. The internal tug of war began. I wanted to have a close, personal relationship with Christ and I knew He tests us by challenging us to obey Him. It costs us nothing to be saved but it costs everything to follow Him. When the requirements of what he asks of us seem too daunting, too lofty or too dangerous we run or become paralyzed. However, I *did* share my testimony on discipleship and my panic disorder. It was freeing and terrifying at the same time, but I felt alive again. I was finally using my gifts for the Lord." Eventually she learned that God gave us the Bible to help us walk through our fears and face them... not to avoid and escape them.

What caused this transformation? Jan shared two truths to encourage Dawn. The first was that God looks at her heart and so would the women. "It won't matter if you stumble, falter or even faint," Jan said. "They will see your love for God and your passion for Him. *That* will be powerful." Secondly, Dawn's role was just to deliver God's message. He would be the center of attention — not her. Those truths lightened Dawn's heart and helped her focus on God's will, rather than her comfort. This was a victory, but it still took years to be set free from captivity (Isaiah 61:1-3).

The second challenge brought panic to her soul when she was asked to donate blood for a child.

Dawn has O negative blood, which is relatively rare. She knew it was clean because she had no drug use, no sexual diseases and had not been infected by the hepatitis B or C virus. She volunteered to give blood to a child in need. After her blood was drawn she hyperventilated and swore to never donate blood again. Less than two weeks later, she was asked to give again and agreed. But as the day approached, Dawn grew terrified and experienced the worst panic attack of her life. Dave thought she was going to have a heart attack. In the relentless battle to control her thoughts, her mind raced with negative and stinging accusations of cowardice. By morning, she was sick to her stomach. Dave held her and encouraged her with Romans 8:36-37. She could not be separated from the love God had for her.

"God's desire for me to conquer my fears is not based on the idea that He will revoke His love for me, but rather that He desires me to live my life to the fullest... complete in Him. God used that event to change my life once more. I resolved that whatever it took I would leave no stone unturned in finding out the cause of these attacks and to overcome them."

"I swallowed my pride and spoke with my doctor, who recommended a psychiatrist, and I began taking medication. Though I was not opposed to medication, as it had helped family members, I just *really* did not want to see a psychiatrist. After all, what would people think? Would this jeopardize my husband's ministry? I was very concerned about both mine and my husband's reputation."

Dawn learned that God heals and is the Lord over those who are healed. "He also showed me I never have to be ashamed of the testimony that comes from His hand. I didn't need to fret over His reputation or what others may think."

Dawn saw a psychiatrist who prescribed two medications, which worked poorly for her. She then saw a Christian counselor who taught her deep breathing, which people with panic disorders rarely do. The breathing technique took two weeks before she saw relief. Dawn also looked into EMDR (Eye

Movement Desensitization and Reprocessing), and she took Jan with her to appointments to help discern if this form of treatment was even Biblical.

"I learned being godly does not mean I am void of emotions, even those like anger and fear," Dawn says. "They are part of being human and were God-given, but not to be stuffed. They are to be dealt with and used for His glory." She learned to look at things from God's perspective. "I looked at Bible characters and realized they also had faults. God used them anyway; not because they were perfect, but because they believed in Him."

One night, while attending a worship service, Dawn prayed about her dream to leave her field of employment and stay home. Just a year later, Mt. Gilead Camp offered her a position to work alongside her husband. She says it was one of the happiest days of her life. Dawn serves as his assistant and also coordinates Women's Ministries at the camp. God heard her and gave her a good gift. "Although I truthfully deserve nothing," she says, "as His precious child He has given me the precious right to dream big. He is able to bring things to pass that have been designed for us to do. Ask. He will hear and answer in His way and in His time."

"The Lord has impressed upon me that integrity, love, transparency, dependence on God, accountability, compassion and absolute commitment to God's Word must characterize this ministry. Earlier, four of these traits would have been missing from my list. It is only through God's refining process — His transformation — that I have seen the great need for humility, transparency, dependence on God and compassion. Panic became the means by which God would work His great work. I still have not conquered all my fears." Dawn no longer takes medication, but is grateful that it was available. She no longer feels like a captive to her fears, and does not berate herself when she does cave in to fear. She tries to keep a steady gaze on Jesus who loves her regardless.

"I've learned through these years that the Lord's love may look different than we like," Dawn says. "In the book, *The Lion, the Witch and the Wardrobe*, one of the children asks another character about Aslan. 'Is Aslan safe?' The other character responds, 'No he isn't safe, but he is good.' God has taught me that His way is not always safe and comfortable, but it is good and it is best and it results in God being glorified."

God has used the testimony of Dawn's transformation, brought about through His strength and power. God helped Dawn to overcome her weaknesses while enabling her to share her story with others. Many have come with tears and shared their stories of depression, anxiety and other emotional trials. God has also used Dawn's testimony as a catalyst to bring freedom to many and enable them to no longer hide or pretend that their struggles do not exist. As they come out of hiding, they take the first step in finding healing.

"Ministry is following in the footsteps of the saints of old. To serve our great God, allow Him the *right* to transform you as His vessel — inside out and backwards, if that is what it takes — to accomplish His plan and purpose for your life. To answer when He calls with, *'Here I am, your servant, for I will do all that you ask of me even if I am afraid, still I will trust in you,'* (Italics mine). Those who respond to this call have the privilege of being used to change the world for Christ and through Christ."

Dawn's resolve to walk through this phobia is found in the strength of Christ. When every fiber within her body desires to run and avoid fearful situations, Dawn now takes steps to maintain a steadfast gaze upon her Lord. Rather than fear things of this earth, she walks through it with Christ. Dawn knows that He is with her wherever she is and loves her, regardless of her performance. So, whether she drives over a bridge or not, or takes a flight or not — the Lord's love for her never diminishes. His unchanging love has transformed her life, providing her with a solid sense of safety and security. It took many years before she settled into this haven of acceptance.

Dawn, a transformed vessel, sought God and He healed her not — instantly, but over the course of many years. He used her hurts to build her character and then to build others up. God never changes. He is the same today, tomorrow and forever; He will not let you down.

How about you? Maybe you don't suffer panic attacks, but are you fearful? Are you hiding from the Lord and others because of it? Won't you follow Dawn's example by trusting and leaning on Him? What do you have to lose except the issue brothering you? God did not let Dawn down and He will not let you down either. Remember, *"Trust in the Lord with all your heart and lean not on your own under-standing"* (Proverbs 3:5, Italics mine).

Joy — Hand Sculpted

Romans 8:28-29; 2 Corinthians 5:17-20a;
Ephesians 1:13-14

J oy serves the Lord as a missionary now, but the
road she traveled has been long and hazardous.
The Beatles' song, "The Long and Winding Road,"
has become the theme of her life. The journey literally seemed to be long, endless and terrifying.

Despite how bright my friend is and how hard
she tried to achieve academically and athletically,
Joy struggled against an empty ache inside her. Even

though she had become a child of God early in her life and grew up with a Christian family, something got lost between their words and their practice of faith.

Joy was born with a cleft palette during the era where resources other than surgery for her condition were limited. She endured thirty-one surgeries plus five years in speech therapy to try and repair her mouth and lip, but not before her birth defect set her up as a target for ridicule by those that did not understand. Her classmates constantly ridiculed her appearance and the way she spoke, especially during the late elementary school years.

One day Joy came home in tears and her mother asked her what was wrong. Joy told her mom about the insults, teasing and harassment she had experienced that day at school. Her mother called the school principal. He confronted the children Joy had named, who denied any wrongdoing. The principal called her mother back saying that Joy must have lied.

A new level of pain ensued. A mother's influence penetrates deep. Joy realized this when her mother believed the words of the principal and children over her own daughter. "Never come home with stories like that one again," she chided. This one statement started the process of internal sculpting that made Joy believe that she was not as valued as the other children. It was the ultimate of insults. Joy learned to internalize all her hurt feelings. She also chose to honor her mother's wish.

This resulted in Joy feeling alone, unprotected and over the course of time, she became depressed. Self-blame also developed as she tried to rationalize the event and came to believe it all stemmed from her birth defect. Embarrassed and trying to hide the defect, Joy developed a habit of covering her mouth with her left hand when she spoke.

At the time Joy did not understand the full impact of her mother's words or the reason for her treatment towards her. This led her to question what her parents thought about their own child. What she couldn't understand as a young girl was that maybe this had more to do about their childhood than hers.

Later, when Joy became an adult, she discovered her mother had been abandoned as a child. She also discovered her father had been dramatically orphaned and separated from most of his siblings. As parents, did they ever consider the impact of their early childhood and how it might affect their own children? Unfortunately, early childhood trauma, left unattended and treated, may have negative effects on a parent-child relationship. Unbeknownst to them, their childhood scars affected their parenting and their hurting daughter.

Joy absorbed all the harsh words, threats and name calling and they became her reality. For sculpted on her heart was the message, "Defective; not good." She had to work through her childhood scars before she would be mentally healthy. Joy suffered from depression. At one point it became so severe that she was hospitalized in the Minirith and Meier Clinic for treatment. "Those years were terrible enough." Much like the sculptors pick and chisel, negative and hurtful words leave their mark on children who are unable to discern truth from error. Unfortunately, those messages developed into a sense of self-loathing yet God used them to mold her heart to feel tenderness and acceptance for others who were also "different."

Joy's acceptance and compassion for the "unloved" and those who appear different came to light recently when a former middle school friend told her, "The reason we always followed you around at lunch was because we felt accepted. We were the outcasts and, like Jesus, you accepted us."

They called her a "female-Billy Graham." Joy's eyes filled with tears as she came to a realization. "God," she prayed, "You used me even then to show Jesus to others." It was God's purpose to show Christ through her to her school friends.

Still, she could not seem to shake her feelings of being unacceptable to others, especially to her mother. Joy concluded that her birth defect was the cause of her misery and trouble. Those lies led to her feeling of worthlessness and depression. Although her later realization did not help her at the moment, later in life, Joy realized her mother probably also struggled with feelings of guilt, even possibly blaming herself for her daughter's condition. Regardless of the circumstances of her birth or life, God had other plans for the child born who appeared to be less than perfect.

Although these were hard times, Joy says that God has blessed her with many friends who supported her at various points throughout her adult life. "Through my many trials," she says, "I always knew God allowed them to teach and mold me into an instrument He could use. Eventually, my life became stable and I began living a 'good' Christian life. I was involved in ministry at church; I had a great and good paying job; and I had a supportive friend. In fact it was so good, I relaxed and let life slide along."

Then, in July of 2003, Joy's cousin challenged her move to another level in her walk with the Lord. As a result of that encounter, her focus changed. "I began to see how selfish I was in not pursuing my former passion to work with deprived children," Joy reflects. "I sought the Lord and purposed in my heart to never go back to sliding through life again. I want to continue to grow in the Lord and to serve."

In 2005, God called Joy to go to an orphanage in the Ukraine where her cousin's family served. She learned that she would work with children who have physical, mental and emotional disabilities. The medical and mental health care resources in these facilities were limited and inadequate. These children did not know Jesus or know that the God who sculpted them loves them.

Joy's cousin had challenged her to walk in a deeper way with the Lord, and Joy accepted it because she knew she could be of use to the children. A new journey was about to take place. Mentally, she was already bound for the Ukraine.

She began the necessary preparations, including gathering information on the orphanage structure. She discovered that the children are evaluated on mental, not physical, abilities and then assigned a level according to the outcome of the assessment. The children of Level One are very bright. Level Two identifies the less intelligent children who are also afflicted with mild physical disabilities; Level Three is for children with mental handicaps; and Level Four is for the severely physically handicapped children. The orphanage caregivers called level four a "death camp" because those children had been left there by their families to die.

Much transpired between Joy, her cousin and the family, during the six months as they served together in the Ukraine. Because of the deep friendship which developed with her cousin, some misunderstandings arose. Some family members may have viewed this relationship as a possible threat or triggered some feelings of insecurities. This, too, was God's hand pointing to her internal sculpting as a child. He wanted to heal her by replacing her old way of coping with a new and healthier way.

After being in the Ukraine for only six months, Joy returned to the U.S. broken and confused, but still determined to finish the work God had started. She was in need of raising more financial support, but there was a bigger reason behind her coming home only God knew. She sought biblical help and allowed God to do the things He does best — release her from her own prison of discouragement. The prophet Isaiah wrote that Jesus came to *"...bind up the brokenhearted, to proclaim liberty to captives and freedom to prisoners... to comfort all who mourn... giving them a garland instead of ashes... So they will now be called oaks of righteousness, the planting of the LORD, that He may be glorified"* (Isaiah 61:1-3, Italics mine).

Joy states, "Without realizing it, I had lowered my guard against the lies that Satan had planted within me throughout my life. At various times I have suffered from depression and struggled with the lies from people and various experiences. I had allowed the opinions of others to trigger my old feelings of poor self-worth rather than realizing who I am in Christ. Because many of those people did not warrant having a say in my life — but I gave them that authority — even though over the years I had learned not to give that authority away, but to cling to who I am in Christ and see myself through God's eyes. Unfortunately, I once again, let a mere man devalue me. By entertaining this person's opinion, it allowed Satan to sneak into my thoughts and rob me of my value. It even got to the point that I was convinced that I had no value, and everyone would be so much better off without me. Satan is so subtle and so conniving; I didn't see it coming. I didn't see a lot of things until I actually arrived home and started to work through the events that led up to the point of my wanting to call it quits."

Joy believes it is imperative to know where the believer's true worth and value is found, in Jesus. This is every believer's assurance, for when erroneous accusations and opinions assail us we will not entertain the lie. Believers who have trained their minds on God's truth will always evaluate and filter other's views and opinions through Scripture. If it proves untrue, we take *"...every thought captive to the obedience of Christ,"* as 2 Corinthians 10:5 commands (Italics mine). Then, we can exchange the lie for the truth according to the Romans 12:2 mandate, *"Be transformed by the renewing of our mind"* (Italics mine).

Joy found herself waiting upon God. "Growing up in a Christian home, I had always heard, *'Wait upon the Lord,'* (Italics Mine). This year, I have had to live out those words in my everyday life. Although I recognize that if it were not for all the experiences that have occurred throughout my life, I would have never learned how faithful God is, and how much He cares for me. So, certainly I can wait on Him to take me back to the children in the Ukraine."

As Joy was waiting on God another trial began to see if she really trusted Him. It started with her feeling unsettled. God uprooted her for the second time, calling her to leave her home, church and friends; this time to go back to Pennsylvania. Without complaining or questioning, she followed His lead.

Although life was not easy back there and various trials ensued (unemployment and dwindling finances, which in the past had previously lead her into depression) she experienced a sense of freedom. That led her to release within her soul all her past insecurities, poor self-view and self-doubt. She was free from the past at last, because of His marvelous grace and love. Now she was ready to begin making inquiries about returning to the Ukraine.

Just because God heals does not mean we will not struggle with negative emotions or thoughts again. As Joy was contemplating returning to the Ukraine, old feelings for acceptance resurfaced and left Joy in a vulnerable state. This was a time of testing for Joy. She decided not to allow the old feelings to control her; instead she used them as a catalyst to remind her of His grace and her deep affinity for the children at the orphanage. She knew she could return to the Ukraine, healed of her many old wounds and insecurities, even if some residue still existed. She recognized her choice to either give in to them or overcome them. This knowledge gave her a new sense of freedom in Christ.

Armed with this new awareness, Joy decided to contact the mission agency and ask for another chance. She received an open door to return. Joy took a short-term trip back to the Ukraine and God re-ignited her passion and love for this work. The negative influence was no longer a problem. Her future plans are to return to the Ukraine and serve for two years. When this transpires, she will then seek God's direction for a longer stay, hopefully leading to a permanent post. Until that takes place she has relocated to another city and job that is open to her going back on the mission field.

God continues to test Joy with lessons He has taught her. At times she struggles with insecurity, but it has not defeated nor incapacitated her. In fact, Joy has become quite bold in the pursuit of righteousness. She lovingly took a risk and confronted her cousin. God's hand was on this situation and the fruit that came forth was a commitment to be a watch guard for each other's purity and righteousness. Her relationship with her cousin is alive and well. They are not only cousins, but good friends.

Towards the end of her short-term stay at the orphanage, Joy's heart yearned to leave something of value with these children. She taught them the song "Jesus Loves Me" using sign language. One little boy said, "Now I can teach my parents this song. They are both deaf."

God took Joy's previous sculpting — the shaping that came through human opinions and words — and He remolded and shaped her. He turned the scars from her old feelings of abandonment, rejection, disfigurement, depression and the history of her parent's neglect into His special work of art. Joy is an example now of compassion, kindness and trust.

The Psalmist tells us that God molds or sculpts in the womb of our mother. Joy's cleft palette was no surprise to Him. He created her and used her life experiences to shape her heart and compassion for those born like her. She came to see that all children, regardless of how they look, are created and born with inherent value.

Only the Creator can take a piece of defective clay and sculpt it into something beautiful. God designed and molded a special person for a special ministry. He called Joy to serve children who are "different;" "outcasts" in the world. Through God allowing Joy to suffer rejection, He enabled her to understand and relate to those children who had been ostracized by their family and society. Now she travels internationally so that she can minister to other rejected children. God turned my friend's experiences of rejection, harassment and abandonment into a useful tool for His glory.

God used Joy not only for His glory, but also for the well-being of those children in the Ukraine orphanage. Joy's deep need for acceptance has been completely met through the Lord and His Word in her inner being. Now her life is full of dreams, hopes and aspirations to touch orphaned children. Joy discovered that her true significance couldn't be removed, devalued or withheld because it comes from God.

Joy likes to share Psalms 139:1-16: *"... Behold, O Lord, Thou dost know it all. Thou hast enclosed me behind and before, and laid Thy hand upon me. Such knowledge is too wonderful for me... Thy right hand will lay hold of me"* (Italics mine).

The Bible is clear that mankind came into being through God. In Genesis 1:26-31, God establishes that he sculpted Adam from clay by His own hand. He created the universe and then fashioned humanity in His image. This truth, penned in Psalm 139:15-16, states that He *"skillfully wrought"* each person (Italics mine).

But His work doesn't stop there. For the willing person, God hand-sculpts the heart and the soul. He shapes his or her future. He takes His chisel and turns the raw material of our lives into something beautiful and useful. God, in all His wisdom and creativity, offers a permanent hope and promise of freedom to all who will seek Him. He is the only one who can. Have you had the opportunity to watch the Master Sculptor transform a friend or relative? Have you watched Him change... you?

Emma — From Plastic to Porcelain

(Joshua 1:3; Psalm 94:19;
Jeremiah 18:2-4; Romans 12:1-2; 1
Corinthians 10:5; 2 Corinthians 4:7;
Philippians 4:6-9, 10-15; Colossians 3)

Emma is a close friend of mine who grew up in an environment of "passive influence." This is a situation where there is poor or little positive inter-action, leaving a lasting negative effect on children. Passive influence can take place through half-hearted gestures, the omission of kind words and actions or no words at all — simply looks and gestures that cause one to believe the worst about oneself.

Emma received much affection from her father and grandfather, but demeaning actions and words from her mother stripped them away and left her with no sense of worth and value. Her inner core became warped by confusion, insecurities, guilt and a wrong view of herself as a person. Unfortunately, the effects of this negative passive influence can lay seemingly dormant until suddenly cued, taking its victim right back to where it all began. This type of influence tears at the very core of a person's being. Emma remembers her mother telling her that she loved her, while her face looked hateful, even murderous. This type of communication is dubbed as "double-binded," leaving a person confused, with a wrong view of herself. The exchange between Emma and her Mother left behind a wake of confusion; she was constantly questioning what her mother really meant.

Rather than building her up, Emma's childhood drilled holes into her soul until she was unable to be real with herself or with others. Today's teens would have described her as "plastic." In other words, she was not "real," but malleable, becoming anything that anyone may have wanted her to be; anything other than who she really was.

Emma began her life as the "apple" of both her father and grandfather's eyes. This created within her a sense that she could do no wrong; she literally believed she could "walk on water." Unfortunately, the ones who regarded her so highly would not be around for long.

Emma's grandfather died, leaving her with a deep sense of loss and feeling very alone. As was typical of her home life, Emma was left adrift to deal with her loss. Sadly, the adults in her family were so consumed in grief and funeral responsibilities that they overlooked her. Mrs. Jensen, a teacher at her school, tried to comfort her. She took Emma out of the classroom and held her, helping her to cry over her loss. Other than her teacher, Emma was left to walk her journey of grief alone. She did not have an opportunity to say goodbye to her grandfather because he died during the night, and she was not permitted to attend the funeral. Her parents never explained this decision, but it's likely they either thought they were protecting her or were not handling well their own loss. It would be forty years later, when her own father died, before she felt the closure and peace she needed.

As a child, Emma attended Vacation Bible School (VBS) each summer. Aunt Grace made Emma feel so loved that it permeated her very soul so that even today she feels that love. Emma was always encouraged to attend Sunday school by those who taught VBS. She would have good attendance for a few weeks but then her attendance would taper off because her help was needed on the family farm. She did manage to memorize the twenty-third Psalm through Sunday school, and it became an integral part of her being. Growing up, she would thumb through her Bible searching for that passage when she needed peace for her hurting soul.

Death soon visited this family again when Emma's grandmother died. During her grandmother's illness, Aunt Grace convinced the grandmother to make her the sole beneficiary of her will, even though Emma's father had been the one living on and maintaining the family property. Emma's father was devastated by the double loss; both his mother and land. He began drinking heavily, trying to numb his pain as easily as possible. This passive influence left tension in the home which Emma chose to ignore. Her mother tried to keep things together despite the chaos.

When Emma was just fifteen, her mother looked to Emma for marital advice because she was desperate over their marital discord. Although Emma had not seen her father drunk or heard her parents argue, she was tired of the tension in the house and told her mother to kick her father out. She thought that with only one parent at home, she might have more freedom. Emma's mother did decide to ask her father to leave and then held her daughter fully responsible for the separation. Her mother's accusatory and unforgiving nature weighed heavy on Emma

Shortly after her father left, Emma's aunt went to her high school and had her summoned; her father needed her. With her heart racing and feelings of impending doom washing over her, Emma rushed to his home and found him thrashing, moaning and crying out for help. The teen unknowingly witnessed a man suffering withdrawals from alcohol addiction. That frightening scene left her confused and concerned. Her confusion only grew when her mother showed up, angry that Emma had been taken anywhere without her permission.

Emma's father was admitted to a detoxification center and she could only visit him once a week. Unfortunately, the image of him in weakness and vulnerability changed their relationship forever. She now saw him as a man broken in heart, mind and spirit, and he was humiliated that his special girl had seen him in such a state.

A year later, he remarried a woman with four children, and the father who made her feel like she was the "apple of his eye" was gone. Any opportunity to rebuild a relationship with her father was now overshadowed by his new wife's insecurities. She perceived Emma to be a threat and could not share his affection with anyone, not even his daughter. Emma didn't understand it at the time, but in his absence, she began to seek attention from men.

Emma took care of her siblings while her mother worked two jobs. Because she was only a teen and not a fully responsible adult, she often left her siblings alone to enjoy good times with her friends. She dated a senior boy who seemed like a gentleman until one night when he tried to take advantage of her. She was able to fight him off, but the experience put her sharply on guard. She determined that in the future, she would be the one in control, especially where men were concerned.

Emma began dating Joe. He had graduated from school and was called to serve in the Vietnam War. While he was gone she dated another fellow. Obviously, Joe was quite unhappy to return home and discover Emma's unfaithfulness. They had many fights, and Emma figured it was the end of the relationship.

Emma was not aware that her mother was working in the background to reunite Emma and Joe.

She knew Joe loved Emma and believed he would provide well for her daughter. Deep inside, Emma knew this was a mistake, but she agreed to reconcile and marry Joe. The idea of a wedding and marriage seemed too romantic to miss. After all, her mother could barely make ends meet for her three girls even with two jobs, and Emma missed having a significant male in her life. Joe wanted her.

Joe and Emma married and moved to a small town where Emma felt isolated and alone. Far from her family and friends, she had no way to communicate or visit them. She was without a phone, car or bus service. After only four months of marriage, Emma convinced Joe they should start a family. She hoped that a baby would abate her loneliness and provide Joe with a purposeful focus.

Emma discovered that Joe returned from serving in Vietnam with some emotional and psychological baggage. He turned to alcohol to self-medicate his post-war stress, and their relationship deteriorated into domestic violence. It started with verbal abuse but escalated into physical abuse.

Emma wanted a baby more than ever, thinking it could save her marriage. She became pregnant, but rather than solving their marital problems, this new responsibility caused Joe's bad behavior to grow. He attempted to strangle her. Emma's mother quickly gave Emma permission to move back home.

But Joe continued to harass and stalk her. The police had to be called on numerous occasions. Joe eventually resigned himself to the fact that Emma was out of his life forever. He filed for divorce and also gave up parental rights to their baby girl. Many years later, Emma could see how God's hand of grace protected her from a very dangerous man. Joe eventually committed suicide after killing his third wife.

Even though Emma experienced the hardship of being a single mom, she was able to finish beauty school and begin a career. During this time she met and began living with a young man she knew from high school. He claimed to be religious but his actions proved otherwise. He lived piously on the weekends, going to church and confessing his sins, but during the week, he was out of control.

He yelled at Emma telling her that she would go to hell, because she would not forgive him for his weekly escapades. Her heart hardened towards all men and towards God. It seemed "hypocritical" to Emma, after watching this man confess and proclaim that God would forgive him, that He would appear to refuse to fix her broken heart. Emma says, "One day I decided that if I was going to go to hell, as he said, I might as well enjoy myself and have fun on my way." They split, and Emma began dating again.

She met a young man, Peter, at a local tavern. They connected and he moved in with her. He was different from the other guys she dated. He was younger, educated, and held convictions — some of which he did not always live by — such as living with a woman to whom he was not married. Yet after four years, their togetherness was thin and their inner conflict took its toll on the relationship. Unbeknownst to them, God was about to use the death of Peter's grandmother to intervene and transform their lives from plastic to porcelain.

When Peter's grandmother died, his father came out to the Pacific Northwest to attend the funeral. Peter's father heard that his son was living with a gal to whom he was not married. Disappointed in his son's choices, his father withheld the inheritance that his grandmother had left him. He could not, in good conscience, condone his son's poor behavior and choices.

It has been said if you cannot see God's hand in your life, you ought to be able to see His heart. Peter's mother had already confronted Peter about his living arrangement. Emma had found this odd, as her family would have encouraged the decision. They believed "no commitment — no loss and no pain." Weren't they just two people trying to meet each others needs? What was the big deal? Their "family" — Peter, Emma and Rachel, the daughter from her previous marriage — was just harmlessly helping each other, right?

The next Christmas, God began to stir Peter's heart. He asked himself how he could be a role-model for this little girl, Rachel, who did not even know the true reason for Christmas. To lower his guilt for leading Emma into an unmarried lifestyle, Peter decided to send Rachel to a private Christian school. Rachel heard the gospel, believed and accepted Jesus as her Savior. From that moment on, when the class gathered in a circle to pray, Rachel prayed that her mom and Peter to would come to know Jesus.

God stirred the pot again. Peter, Emma and Rachel, who was now in the third grade, began occasionally attending a small church with friends. They began searching the "why's" of life. God reminded Emma of Psalm 23 and brought to her the realization that when she was a hurting child she found comfort in this Psalm. She also remembered a vow she made to God: she would raise her children in a "religious home."

The pastor's children attended the same school as Rachel. This opened doors for Emma and the pastor's wife to interact at school functions, and soon, she invited Emma to attend a Bible study. One week, the leader at this study asked, "If you were at the gates of Heaven, why should you be allowed in?" Emma burned with wonder as the group provided several wrong answers. The pastor shared with Emma how Jesus Christ died for her and that entrance to Heaven is only through His blood. He talked about a love that did not match any type of love Emma had ever experienced — a love with no strings attached.

As Emma headed home with a heavy heart, her eyes were opened to see the destructive path she had been walking. Nothing could numb her pain. Several nights after hearing the gospel, she got down on her knees and cried out to God. Emma knew within herself that her life had changed, even if she could not comprehend salvation's full meaning. She experienced great peace, like what is described in the Gospel of John, chapter fourteen. Emma took the next step and contacted both the pastor and his wife. She began Bible study and counseling with them.

Peter, meanwhile, was working temporarily in another state. Emma began to write to him and share what had transpired in her life. He understood this eternal transformation better than she realized. When he returned home, Emma informed him that they no longer could live together unmarried. Peter was devastated. Since she had not yet obtained an apartment for her and Rachel to live, Emma took a small room at the YWCA while Rachel stayed with Peter. Emma looked for a suitable apartment and visited Rachel every day.

Peter used her visits with Rachel to attempt to convince her to move back in with him, but Emma withstood his manipulation. One day she informed him that they *both* knew it was a sinful relationship, and she could no longer be a part of it. In that moment, Peter found himself at the end of his road. His little family was crumbling, and he was unable to stop its demise. Emma suggested he contact the pastor. Peter wrestled with God internally but after a few days bent his knee to the Lord Jesus Christ.

Now a new man in Christ, Peter desired to win Emma back. He contacted her, told her what had transpired and asked if he could attend Easter service with her. As Peter and Emma walked out of church that fateful Sunday, Emma's hard heart softened to this man walking beside her. Not only was her heart changed, but a new love for him, the love of Christ, filled her very being.

Several days later Peter sought Emma's hand in marriage. They called his mother to share their new life in Christ and to tell her that they were finally going to be married. Peter's mother got to see the fruit of all those years when she prayed for Peter and Emma's salvation.

They married six weeks later. As they stood before family and friends, they desired to demonstrate that they were committing their lives *first* to the Lord. They wanted the focus on their Savior because of His love and His forgiveness for sins. They began their married life as a means to exhibit God's redemptive process.

Twenty-five years later, Emma and Peter still hold these values. God gave Emma a man who demonstrates trust and commitment, something she lacked in her childhood and other relationships. Before she knew Christ she was not able to trust anyone. Proverbs 3:5-6 says, *"Trust in the Lord with all your heart and do not lean not on your own understanding. In all your ways acknowledge Him and He will make your paths straight"* (Italics mine). Emma discovered that with Christ as their guide, both she and Peter could share a meaningful, lifelong relationship.

Emma had been on a destructive pathway, searching for a meaningful purpose. She was unaware that her search would lead her on such a dangerous course until she met the one who gave her life. Christ entered and led her in a new direction — one of hope, love, forgiveness and grace. He offered her what she had always wanted — total acceptance of her, warts and all. Emma's life changed, and she continues to move forward with her Lord. She discovered that once she yielded to Him, He breathed new life into her. He transformed her into a brand new person, a "porcelain masterpiece." (Emma would not say this about herself, but as her friend who loves and respects her, I can!) Through a long and hard process of change, God allowed Emma to see herself more and more through His eyes.

Once plastic, or to put it another way, an ever-changing chameleon, Emma has found true stability. She understands she was intimately created by God, chosen by Him and is a sister to Christ. These truths give her great security. Even though Emma still struggles sometimes with previous influences, she relies on the Bible to keep her focused on Jesus and His promises. She is excited to know that He will complete His good work in her.

"God uses the picture of a lump of clay, saying, "He is the 'Potter'," she explains. "He will use people and circumstances to remove impurities until He has a beautiful porcelain vessel made for His purposes and use — which *He* planned and *He* created."

God has also brought godly women into Emma's life to help her in her walk with Him. One of these godly women was her Sunday school teacher, Mrs. Jensen, the same teacher who encouraged her when she was a little girl and hurting. Emma ran into this sweet lady while attending a Christian training seminar. Emma shared her story and thanked her for the love that she showed and its permeating influence throughout Emma's life over thirty-five years ago.

Emma recently felt God lead her to share her story, hoping it can touch other women. "It is not easy reliving a life you would like to bury," she says. "But the scars I carry from my childhood and young adult years are nothing compared to the scars Jesus carries because of me. He gave His life for me, and I must be willing to give my all back to Him." Though it was a hard process for her, she submitted. "God used godly women in my life to help me with my walk; how could I not do the same?"

Emma's purposeful and permeating influence has been impacting children and women ever since her encounter with Christ. Emma, once just a glob of clay, is now transformed. Like clay, she had to go through many firings and sandings in order to become a valuable piece of porcelain. God, The Potter, molded her into a beautiful woman and a vessel of great worth in His kingdom, transformed because of God's "purposeful influence." Her story is one of encouragement as we have watched her struggle, fall, get up and continue to grow in Christ-like qualities. Praise be to our God, who restores and resurrects His own!

Is anything preventing *you* from being changed? What in your life is getting in the way of allowing God to mold you from a porous piece of clay (with many impurities) into a precious work of art? Only the Master Potter is able to accomplish such a feat. Will you let Him?

Grams — From a Hope Chest to a Treasure Chest

Colossians 1:5; 2 Thessalonians 2:16

My Grams was one of those women the Lord placed in the life of her grandchildren, allowing her to influence each one's soul. Her influence helped to solidify their core values of God, country and family. Grams instilled a strong work ethic in her children and into those grandchildren who had the privilege of living close to her. As was often the case in the late 1800's, most women did not have the luxury of a formal education. Though some might say Grams was uneducated she demonstrated wisdom, finesse and managerial skills that would match any CEO today. She did this by rearing her seven children almost totally without the help of her husband; she sewed all the family's clothing, took in the neighbors' laundry and ironed — all while running a boarding house which provided for her family's needs. Grams placed much treasure in the hearts of those who loved and respected her. Her Christian faith was evident in all she did.

My Grams, Ida Ann Hazelwood, was born to Molly Horseman Hazlewood Nichols on June 9, 1870, in Pocahontas, Arkansas. She died just before her seventy-fifth birthday. She was a thin, yet stately woman, who stood tall. When Grams let her hair down it fell past her waist. She would pull it back and twist it into a bun, held in place by two long tortoise shell hairpins; this was the way she always wore it. Some people may have seen her stature as intimidating while others were uncertain about whether to like her or not. Though her demeanor appeared stoic to some, to me she was warm, heartfelt and caring.

Grams' life was hard from the very start. Her mother, Molly, died shortly after her birth. Two different stories floated through our family: my Mom stated that Grams was given to several different foster parents after her mother's death.

Grams, however, had a different story. She told me that after her mother died, her father remarried. Much like the sad story of Cinderella and the wicked stepmother, Grams worked around the house like a servant girl and her father did not intervene. The harsh treatment came to an abrupt climax when Grams was thirteen. Apparently her stepmother thought that Grams had been mouthy to her. The woman beat her for three hours, hoping to break Grams' spirit. When the beating was over, Grams would not retract her words. However, the abusive plan backfired; Grams left that home not with her spirit broken, but with a will of iron.

As a result of the beating, Grams left home. She told me that after leaving she lived in a teepee with a Native American Medicine Woman who cared for her, taught her about herbal medicine and imparted other wisdom and information that Grams used the rest of her life. When Grams was old enough to fend for herself, she moved to Little Rock, Arkansas, and became a professional seamstress.

From the time she was beaten until the day she died Grams' jaw was set like flint; she was a very determined lady. Though some found her to be cold, leaving them to draw the conclusion that she was unemotional — I know my mother saw her that way, her grandchildren saw her differently. We saw her as loyal, willing to share her time, giftedness, life and experiences, always pointing us in the right direction.

Grams' true early life may be a bit murky, but to her grandchildren, the important things were clear. She brought us joy and refuge; she was always available and willing to share her knowledge and skills. She purposely deposited wisdom into her grandchildren, building in each of us a foundation for who she believed we could become.

Sometime after Grams moved to Little Rock, she met and married Hugh Jackson. He was a printer and reporter of a local newspaper which I believe he owned. Grams never thought she would marry; in those days a twenty-three year old single woman was considered an old maid. Grams said Hugh had a "gypsy foot," so sometime in the early 1900s they decided to move to Washington State. They went by wagon train.

One of the stories Grams told happened on the trail. Grams' oldest son had never owned a pair of shoes so she traded a bushel basket of tomatoes to get him some. These were his very first pair of shoes, and when he wore them his feet swelled. My uncle threw them away in exasperation. Grams, as one can imagine, was fit to be tied. It was a long journey ahead of them with limited storage. Their provisions were minimal, and Grams was not one to waste anything.

Their journey took them to Republic, Washington, where Granddad worked for the railroad and was subsequently gone much of the time. It seemed to Grams he was home just long enough to get her pregnant and then would leave until the baby was due to be born. Out of the eight pregnancies seven survived. Grams' only dark-haired little girl died shortly after birth. Grams said that Granddad cut the umbilical cord too soon. I do not think she ever got over that loss. While her husband was gone so often, Grams helped to support the family by taking in laundry. She also ran a boarding house, primarily for the railroad men.

Regardless of his wandering feet and later, a roving eye, Grams remained loyal to her wedding vows that she made before God. She never dated or saw other men, even though at one point Granddad wanted a divorce because he was seeing a woman in another town. Grams flatly refused his request as he had no legal reason he could divorce her. In that day desiring a divorce did not provide the necessary legal grounds for a divorce.

Her character was impeccable. One lesson she taught me well was to forgive and not hold grudges. Although she had suffered much hardship and disappointment from her husband, she never demonstrated bitterness or hate. She taught me to speak my mind but still show compassion. (This lesson requires continual practice on my part.) What made the difference? Christ living in her. Even when she reprimanded me, I had no reason to doubt her love or concern for me. Grams provided me with a sense of security while I was growing up. She somehow always conveyed the message that I was loved. My behavior may not have always been acceptable, but she accepted and loved me as her granddaughter!

I lived close to Grams and spent almost everyday at her apartment. Mom worked Monday through Saturday, so after school I would go to Grams'. When I got older, I had chores to do at home, but still went to Grams' place after completing the chores. I stayed at Grams' until it was time for my radio programs to come on. I never tired of being with her. I was safe and loved, and I see now how she exhibited Christ in every facet of her life. Her very essence permeated my soul, and I thank my Lord daily for her influence.

Subsequently, Grams' apartment became my "boot camp." She was attempting to make her grandchild into a loving and accepting person who thought of others, rather than herself. She may not have been academically smart (she only had a third-grade education), but Grams wisdom exceeded others in so many ways. The wisdom she demonstrated and taught came from Scripture and life experience; she focused on how to treat people who were different in race, culture or beliefs. Her training, at times, was hard but purposeful. At other times, her training seemed rather passive and took on an observational approach with minimal instruction. (She knew what the goal was for our time together.) Much like a sergeant training his men, Grams was preparing me for life.

One important lesson occurred when I was about seven years old, I went to see Grams but she was not home. I snooped in the pantry to find a cookie to eat. My eyes landed on a jar of stewed prunes instead.

My mouth salivated to see my favorite canned fruit, and a battle ensued within me. I gave in to the temptation. I took the jar of prunes like a thief and went home to enjoy this stolen delicacy. When I opened the jar and took a bite of the sweet prunes, they turned bitter in my mouth. Not only did I feel guilty but I could not bring myself to either eat them or go back and face my Grams. That jar stayed on our counter in the kitchen for a long time and eventually molded. When I did go back to Grams' apartment, she met me at the door. Her face showed disappointment and she looked very stern. She said, "If you ever want anything from me, all you need to do is ask." Not only did I get her message — I was embarrassed by my sin. I was crushed in my heart by the look on Grams' face. Even now, when I do something wrong I see Grams' disappointed expression — much like I imagine God's face must look when we sin.

Grams demonstrated an almost prophetic wisdom when, in the early 1950s, Grams' neighbors bought a television set and invited her over one afternoon to watch. Grams watched for only a short period of time before she declared that a television was the "devil's workbox." She warned the ladies that this new invention would keep women from their housework and interfere with the care of home and family. Grams' warning in many ways, proved to be right, but I doubt she had any idea how far-reaching television's impact would become.

Another practical piece of wisdom was imparted to me when I was pregnant with my first child. My Grams sat me down and proceeded to instruct me how to deliver my baby — just in case I did not make it to the hospital. She taught me both with her words of wisdom and through observation how she dealt with various situations. These are only a few examples of the practical wisdom my Grams imparted to me in her lifetime, all of which have continued to impact me greatly.

When it came to her country Grams was a true patriot. She felt it was important to vote and to participate in organizations that supported the United States military. She belonged to both the American Legion Auxiliary and the Veterans of Foreign Wars. I remember her selling poppies for the American Legion during a Memorial Day Parade. The sale of these red crepe paper poppies — made by hospital-ized veterans and disabled veterans — has been an American Legion tradition for over 80 years. The funds helped to provide hospitalized veterans an opportunity to purchase items to give for their loved ones on special holidays.

During the Memorial Day parade Grams stood on the corner of the Main Street and First Avenue selling the poppies from her basket. As the American flag passed by, everyone saluted it except one man.

Grams, of course, noted his action, feeling it was disrespectful to her country and the men that served it. Sometime later that same man happened to knock on her apartment door selling a religious magazine. Grams tersely said to him, "The day you salute the American flag, come back and I will buy a magazine from you." As far as I know, he never did return. My Grams had eyes like an eagle; she missed nothing.

Grams never pushed herself on anyone, and her door was always open to her family and friends. She was frugal, living on a meager income from Granddad's service in the Spanish American War. I believe she also received a small amount from Welfare but cannot be sure as Grams was a proud woman and not one for talking unnecessarily. She kept no charge accounts, and I never heard her complain about not having enough. "Live within your means," she would say. Grams' apartment was in an old smelly building with aged and stained yellow wallpaper with a steep set of stairs to climb. Her apartment was small, but she always gave the impression that it met her needs. I observed her cut out coupons and walk all over town to save a few pennies. As I look back on that time I wish I had been wise enough to pay heed to her frugal discipline. She, like Christ, was an example worth following.

Beyond being a woman to emulate in character, my Grams was a gifted craft person. She was a practical woman who did not have any luxuries as a child. A seamstress by trade, Grams and I would sometimes go to the Goodwill to find clothing she could dismantle and use in new ways. In her hands, useless items became useful. She salvaged material to make dresses and aprons. Small parts were torn into strips to make hooked rugs. One of those rugs lay before her small heater in front of her chair where she would create her crafts. She unraveled old sweaters and rolled each strand into a ball to be later used for knitting wool caps, scarves and baby soakers (old-fashioned rubber pants to go over diapers). Other materials, like flour sacks, became dish towels and pillowcases. My brother, Jack, and I had the privilege of Grams helping us make Mother's Day, birthday and Christmas gifts for our mom. Grams showed us how to stencil and then embroider flowers onto them to make them each special.

In addition to teaching me how to embroider and crochet, Grams taught me how to make home-made patterns cut out of newspapers. After cutting the pattern out, Grams would pin it to the fabric, cut the fabric and sew the article of clothing she had designed. Some of my most cherished posses-sions as a child were the pinafores she made. In fact, she had made her own burial dress using the same technique.

By example, she trained me to be a homemaker. In her day, a woman trained to care for her family and home, much like the Proverbs 31 woman, ready in all seasons. Those skills were regarded as simply part of being a good wife, mother and homemaker. She passed on these homemaking abilities to her daughters and grandchildren. In so doing, each event or new situation became Grams manual for more training. Besides molding her granddaughter with her heart her hands were never idol. Her life exemplified a love for her grandchild, a deep love for godly living and for the Bible.

Grams' legacy to all who knew her was one of faith and integrity. She modeled these things for me, just like the older women in the Book of Titus were commanded to do. She never lied, gossiped or complained about her life or about others. She was a quiet woman who stood up straight, spoke her mind when provoked and had compassion for others, even when she might disagree with them; especially regarding her faith in the Lord, marriage or country.

I am reminded that behind Grams' couch was an enormous hope chest. It housed some of her handiwork along with pictures and important documents that she treasured. Those things were to be handed down to the next generation. I am not sure what happened to the trunk and its treasured contents after Grams had to go to the nursing home and her death. Most likely my uncles and aunts divided its contents. However, I still wish I could have known all the wonders that enormous trunk held.

I most enjoyed her stories and the wisdom she shared during those times of training. Grams' hope was in Christ and the Scriptures; her teaching, like Christ was simple, yet profound. She set a standard for hard work, honesty and integrity. She stood up for her values and beliefs, yet offered compassion to those who tried to twist, confront or demean her code of ethics. She had a hard life without many "pats on the back" but always trusted her Savior and Lord. What a legacy she left behind.

Not unlike the "hope chest" which held her belongings, I have been given a better, more bountiful "treasure chest," filled with her memories, stories and wisdom.

Let us consider what constitutes a treasure. For me, treasures are those experiences — both joyful and sad — where the power and grace of the Holy Spirit allows us to grow. They are memories, stored in our hearts and used to encourage or teach. They are snapshots of character, moments of strength, eras of faith. When we pass our treasures on to others, we ultimately and reproduce ourselves in them.

My Grams did not know that she was reproducing herself in her grandchildren, but that is exactly what she did. By her words and example, she created in us our own hope for the unseen future. She grafted in us the desire to be prepared and to share our treasures with others. She passed on her talents, her integrity, and her insight to forgive. She was the most influential human being to permeate our lives.

What treasure is the Lord trying to build within you? What skills? What insights? What experiences in your life could be shaped and stored by His grace? Don't waste a single moment — won't you give Him permission to make your life a treasure chest?

Sue — Pursuing Love

John 13:34-35, 15:9; I Corinthians 14:1;
Ephesians 5:2

Let me introduce you to a precious sister in the Lord with whom I became acquainted through her children. Her sons are pastors and minister at the church I attend. Her daughter attends as well. I sat in church with her this Sunday as one of her sons preached. Her whole family was there to hear this gifted young man break open the Living Word. Knowing her story and seeing the fruit of her labor through her grown children, I asked if she would be willing to share her story.

Sue's life is one that reflects God's grace and love as she has allowed Him to work through her, enabling her to reach out to those who deeply hurt her. Often children, who are recipients of hurt and pain, even after coming to Christ, are unable or unwilling to mete out the same measure of grace and love that the Lord gave them, but that is not Sue.

Her background is not what most people have experienced. She was born into a Mormon family, and her father was a polygamist. He had eight wives and forty children; the last child was born when he was eighty-two. Sue was her mother's fifth child. The family was poor.

When she was eight years old, the government began cracking down on polygamy and put her father in jail. She endured ridicule and heartache at school because her daddy was a "jail bird." One day she came home from school in so much despair that she cried out for God "to take her home." As Mormon doctrine taught, she believed she would be ushered directly into Heaven when she died because she was a child of God. Eventually, her father was released from jail, and the family moved. Sue made a friend who invited her to a Good News Club. Sue heard the true gospel of Jesus Christ for the first time in her life.

When Sue was thirteen, her sister and polygamous brother-in-law came to visit Sue's family. Unbeknownst to Sue, he was a fugitive, hiding from the police. They invited Sue to travel with them and be their babysitter. Sue had no idea that her brother-in-law had "chosen" her to be his next wife, an "ultimate calling from God" according to the faulty belief system under which she was raised. Sue and her brother-in-law (the polygamist) held hands and prayed (a custom to cement their union) even though the marriage was not consummated.

Sue then returned home and in the following months her sister sent letters to their mother who read them to Sue. Sue's sister was a proverbial Nancy Drew; she wrote messages on the back of her letters in "lemon juice," which were invisible until heated. One message warned Sue that her sister's husband planned to kidnap her. Despite a great sense of fear, Sue penned a letter to him.

As she wrote to break off the marriage, a heavy weight pressed down upon her, and she struggled to breathe. A war began inside her. "I remember I didn't want to do this. I wept as I wrote that letter." Even though the marriage had not been consummated, to break it off was to condemn herself to hell, according to her religious beliefs. "I wanted a husband that loved only me and a home of my own where my kids were able to say, 'This is my father; this is my dad,' rather than calling him by his first name or their uncle. This was the hardest thing I had ever done, yet with a knot in my stomach, I did what had to be done, even though I knew I was committing myself to hell."

When Sue was old enough to leave home, she also left the Mormon Church, an earth-shattering step. By those two decisions, (first to decline marriage to a Mormon man and second to abandon the doctrine she was raised in) she had condemned herself to hell according to the church's view. But, to Sue, the risk was worth it. Her life had already been a living hell. Sexually abused at just three or four years old and emotionally maltreated for years after, Sue had absorbed enough damage. She hoped for something new.

Sue met Rodney at Oregon State College. They married and had three children: two boys and a girl. When the children were four, five and seven, the family began a search to know God. Sue and Rodney noticed a marked change in their neighbors, Loretta and her husband, after they attended a "Marriage Encounter" retreat. Sue and Rodney observed them walking "kind of squishy up and down the road," and thought, "Ah, maybe we'll go, too."

They attended a "Marriage Encounter" weekend. It was a great crash course in communication and both Sue and Rodney came away thinking about two things. First, they needed to know God. Who was He? Second, they wanted a plan for bringing up their kids. Personally, Sue realized she needed to settle concerns regarding her Mormon background.

Sue and her husband went to a local priest seeking answers about God. They told him, "We need to know who God is." The priest answered, "Well, you'll have to pray about it." His unhelpful reply left them frustrated and more confused. If a supposed man-of-God couldn't or wouldn't answer their inquiry, where could they go?

In desperation, they eventually ended up in a little church out in a nearby community. They had expected the pastor to visit them after attending the church, hoping he could help them with their spiritual pursuit. They waited and prayed and finally came a knock on the door. The church pastor *did* come to their home, but they were so busy putting their children to bed that they slammed the door in his face. In fact, this happened several times. Finally, the undeterred pastor took a new approach and called to make an appointment.

Now together, the pastor was able to share about Christ and talk about their spiritual condition. He asked them, "If you died tonight, would you go to Heaven?" Sue answered right away. "Sure." Based upon her Mormon teachings, she believed she was a child of God.

The pastor then shared how sin separates people from God and how Jesus Christ had died on the cross for our sins. He was buried and rose again, becoming the bridge between humanity and God. The pastor quoted John 1:12, *"But as many as received Him, to them He gave the right to become children of God, even to those who believe in His name,"* (Italics mine). Sue's mind began to reel with conflicting thoughts and questions. "I wanted to tell him, 'Get out of here; we have to put the kids to bed!'" However, the seeds of truth had been planted in a fertile heart.

A few days later, Sue sat on her bed praying. "God," she said, "I need to know who you are." She didn't know how He would answer, but the words from John 1:12 came back into her mind. *"But as many as received Him, to them He gave the right to become children of God"* (Italics mine). Sue became fully aware that she had never received Christ and that she was not His child. She found herself confessing her sin and asking for forgiveness. Even though Sue did not understand what sin was, she found herself praying and asking Christ to come into her life and be her Savior and Lord.

Sue met Christ that day. She was so overjoyed that she felt like jumping on the bed. She also felt a strong need to tell somebody what just happened, so Sue went over to her neighbor's house and shared her good news. After hearing how she had prayed, the neighbor told her she did it wrong and should go speak with her pastors. Her pastors came over and also discounted her experience because she had not prayed the "right way." Rather than be discouraged, Sue spoke with great spiritual discernment and asked them to leave. She remarked, "Nobody can take away from your heart what Christ does in there." This confrontation solidified the beginning of Sue's life with her Lord.

Initially, Sue did not have a role model to follow as she lived her life as a mother and wife. She was not aware of how to love her children, and she didn't even know how to clean her house. As a new creation in Christ, Sue began to observe other women and was able to glean from them how to do wifely chores and how to nurture her children.

One of Sue's first memories of God changing her took place during a family camping trip. It was June at Diamond Lake, and the water was very cold. The kids had just come from the lake, wet, shivering and covered in goose-bumps. Previously, Sue would have seen their blue lips and shown little compassion. She might have said, "Buck up. Just get dressed and you'll warm up." Instead, something transpired in her heart and mind that made her want to serve them. They sat on little camp chairs, and Sue brought each of them each a bucket of warm water. Then she fixed them hot chocolate.

Her children enjoyed this new behavior. Her little 4-year old looked at her and said, "Mom, you've changed." Sue knew this was the Lord working in and through her to answer the desires of her heart to be a loving wife and mother. It encouraged her to know first-hand that even without a role model, the Lord could transform her into His vessel of honor. He answered her silent prayer through women who did not realize they were being studied; that is permeating influence.

Sue joined Bible Study Fellowship (BSF) and later became a discussion leader. She led her small group for three years. During that time she prayed over and over her husband would become the spiritual leader in their home. One day while Sue was praying God spoke to her heart. God told her that Rodney couldn't become the leader Sue desired because she had become a stumbling block. Sue listened, prayed and evaluated her commitments and obligations. She wanted so badly for Rodney to take the lead in their marriage and family that she ended up teaching him on leadership, rather than allowing the Holy Spirit to train him.

Sue became enlightened through prayer and the study of Genesis. She could see a discrepancy between the amount of time she studied, prepared and interacted with the women in her small group, versus the time and effort she invested in her husband and family. Although the former was worthwhile, it had become a diversion from her God-given roles as both wife and mother. God led Sue to resign from BSF. With a new determination, Sue began to serve and submit to her mate. As Sue continued to pray for his spiritual growth and leadership, she saw Rodney rise to his role as spiritual leader and a godly husband and father.

Sue continued to study God's word through classes at her church and by listening to teaching tapes. She also took parenting classes to grow into the wife, mother and woman God desired. She concentrated on becoming a better mom, and God answered her prayers.

Sue claimed James 1:5 that told her to ask for wisdom if she needed it. She believed and waited expectantly for the Lord's answer. For instance, Sue needed wisdom to deal with conflict between her and her sons. They would fight, and she would yell at them. Sue desired instead a godly home free from tension so she turned to prayer. "God, help me with this. Go before me; give me Your words. Just help me." His answer came in the mail. She received advice to help her evaluate her relationships: when you're feeling angry, step back; see what's right, what's wrong, and what God would have you do about it. Figure out the consequences. Sue recognized she had a choice. She sat down with her kids and discussed the poor behaviors and attitudes that frequently brought disruption to their home.

That day, her children recognized a different person in their mother, one who would sit and discuss the situation, but also someone who would enforce necessary consequences as well. The children knew their mom would follow through. Sue realized that she, too, had a choice in her behavior. She did not need to yell and scream. Sue chose to no longer respond with anger, and from that day forward, the countenance in her home changed. Coupled with a good relationship with Rodney, Sue's life became a blessing with a good home yielding three children and nine grandchildren who love the Lord.

The pain of Sue's abusive childhood still surfaces to taunt her. Reliving the hurt has sometimes brought disruption to the peacefulness of her home and interfered in her marital union. She finds strength and encouragement through Scripture, implementing

Romans 12:2 to heal and replace her childhood memories. Sue recognized that she was angry with her parents, especially her mom who allowed the abuse to happen. She wanted to face her anger, a natural reaction, and forgive her father so that she could continue to grow in the Lord. Sue prayed for God to help her love both of her parents. Her pursuit of love ensued.

Sue occasionally visited her dad and shared about the Christ of the Bible with him. On one visit, he in turn shared with her. "I went to the Mormon temple," he said, "and saw the demons flying around. It was very scary." Sue recalled quickly that God's Word calls Satan an angel of light. Her father further shared that the Mormon temple rituals were fashioned after the Masonic Lodge. Participants take a vow "to have their throats slit and their guts ripped out" if they revealed temple secrets. Sue felt a shield between them and knew God was protecting her. Her dad continued to tell her that he had already been "translated to his kingdom," where he would become a god. It was so beautiful and the flowers even bowed down to him. He invited her to come to that kingdom to be with him. She needed to pray and follow him.

Sue could not listen any longer. She declared, "I belong to the Lord Jesus, and I won't be coming with you. I need to get out of here." As she stood to leave he invited her to his trailer. "I have your 666 number," he said. Sue responded, "Well, Dad, I belong to the Lord, and I'm not going to have the number of the beast. I love you, but I need to go." She retreated, and her legs could not move fast enough. She drove down the road before pulling over to cry and pray for composure and comfort.

A few years later, Sue was on her way to New York to help her mother-in-law when she received a phone call. Her father was in the hospital. Sue wondered why they called her since there were 600 other possible relatives to notify. She decided to go to the hospital and see if God opened the door for her. She hoped to share the Lord with him one more time. Sue arrived at the hospital early in the morning. Her dad was starting to come out of the anesthetic and seemed tense. Sue rubbed his shoulder, kissed him on the cheek and whispered in his ear. "Dad I love you so much, but I want to be able to see you in Heaven." She shared with him again that in John 14:6, Jesus said, *"I am the way, and the truth, and the life; no one comes to the Father but through Me"* (Italics mine). She told him he needed to receive Christ as His savior and finally prayed with him.

Sue heard a rustling behind her and she turned to see a nurse in the room. "Is there anybody at the hospital who is a Christian?" Sue asked. The nurse answered, "I am." Sue told her, "We come from a big Mormon family, and I'm the only true believer.

If you get the chance would you share Christ with him?" The nurse replied, "I already have."

Sue left and continued her trip to New York. Her father died and although the uncertainty of his eternal destination was difficult, God comforted her heart. The truth of scriptures kept flooding her mind; God created us and He breathed life into us and only He can take that breath away. Nothing is impossible with God, and her father's eternal destiny lies in His hands, along with over 600 other family members. Through this experience with her father, God led her to also look at her mother in a new way.

Over and over again God proved His faithfulness, love and grace to Sue and she relied on it greatly when it came to her mother. As an adult, she could finally realize the deep hatred and blame she projected on her mother, the one she trusted and expected to protect her from harm. Her mother's failure to protect her from blatant abuse seemed unforgivable. "I couldn't stand her to touch me. I couldn't stand to hear her voice on the phone and I was angry," Sue says. "I held a lot against her — more than against the person who abused me — for not protecting me, loving me or nurturing me." This scenario is too often the case involving abuse. Those God placed around us are supposed to protect their children and when they do not, the anger intended for the abuser becomes displaced by being projected onto the parent or other adult responsible for not stepping in and protecting the child.

The Lord convicted Sue through Ephesians 4:30-32. *"And do not grieve the Holy Spirit of God... [but] let all bitterness and wrath and anger... and slander be put away from you, along with all malice... forgiving each other, just as God in Christ also has forgiven you"* (Italics mine). Sue sought God's forgiveness and asked Him to give her His love for her mom. She begged the Lord to show her how to love her mom and to see her as He does. God started changing her heart.

As the years passed, Sue's mother was unable to drive anymore, and Sue took the opportunity to serve the person she once most resented. Sue's mom was skeptical and often asked, "What do you want? What are you here for?" Sue just wanted to love her mother and help her run errands. Like Christ who washed the disciple's feet, Sue wanted to be available to care for her mother's needs, all the while praying for an "open door" to share Christ. Her mother would say, "I just want to die," and Sue would reply, "You are not ready to die." One day, her mother asked, "Why do I need to be ready?"

Sue sent a thank you prayer up to the Lord and said, "Mom, God loves you, and He sent Jesus to die on the cross for your sins. He was buried, and he rose again to give you new life. God's word says, *"But as many as received Him, to them He gave the right to become children of God, even to those who believe on His name"* (John 1:12, Italics mine).

Sue could tell that her mom felt uncomfortable and could sense the spiritual battle going on in her heart. "Mom," Sue said, "you don't have to pray with me. You can do that all on your own because that's a personal relationship between you and God."

Shortly after this, Sue's mother entered the hospital. With all her nearby siblings away at the time, Sue was enabled to be the one who cared for her during her stay. Even though this was a sad situation, it was also exciting. Again her mom lamented, "I just want to die." Sue replied, "Mom you're not ready to die yet. You need to ask Jesus to be your Savior and come into your heart." She said, "I've already done that... a long time ago in my heart." Even though her mother suffered from dementia, Sue believes that her mother couldn't have said this without really knowing Christ. Their relationship grew sweet, loving and centered on Christ. At times, dementia caused her mom to look at Sue without any recognition. During those times Sue held her hands and prayed. The last time Sue looked at her mom, she lovingly said, "Oh Mom, I've been praying for you." Her mother answered, "I know, I can feel it."

Sue is a realist. She cannot say for sure that her mother's final eternal home is with God, but she has placed her trust in Him and His promises. Sue can rest in the knowledge that she shared the gospel of truth with her mom. As a result of Sue's faith in God, neither her mother's dementia nor Satan's lies and taunting were able to create anxiety, fear or doubt in Sue's mind regarding her mother's final eternal destination.

Sue is a faithful woman who loves God. He is the one who has protected her from her enemies and even enabled her to pursue loving relationships with them. God also continues to make Sue into a loving wife for her loving husband. She has embraced submission to him and sees herself as his helper and supporter. Marriage is her opportunity to show him respect.

When Sue meets young women, she encourages them to begin preparing for their future. "Start becoming the woman that God wants you to be for that special person in your life," she says. She loves to see God answer their righteous prayers as they seek Him and grow in knowledge and understanding of the Bible. "Ask questions," she says. "As you read scripture, ask 'What does this say? What does it mean?'"

For women who already have a family to care for, she reminds them of the promise in the book of James and advises them to seek wisdom in every challenge they face. "Remember when you ask in prayer to look expectantly for His answers. They often come in many different ways." Sue firmly believes that

God will grow any woman into the wife and mother He desires her to be, if they are willing to obey Him and willing to give. "Even an older woman confined to her rocking chair can be a blessing," she says. She loves to see women finding ways to encourage other women, through prayer, through phone calls and through practical help.

Sue's pursuit of love, first for God, then for her family and finally for her enemies is a story we can take to heart. As we pursue love, we act in obedience to Jesus (see John 15). Even though none of us ever "arrive," God will continue to work in us and through us so that each day, each month and each year, others will see more of Christ in us. Sue went to Christ for restoration, forgiveness and *His* love to love those who hurt her.

Is there someone in your life who needs that kind of love?

Lorna — Created for Commitment

Genesis 2:20; I Timothy 2: 2-7, 3:11;
Titus 2:3-5; I Peter 4:19

Throughout this book I have shared the personal stories of many women. These women were willing to share their stories of love, hope and ministry along with their struggles and suffering as well. Through it all God is using them for His glory and honor as they influence others for the Kingdom.

Now I make my final introduction: Lorna, my pastor's wife. I have attended the church where she serves for many years and have had the opportunity both to observe her gracious life perspective and also participate in ministry with her. The more I know her and know of her, the more I respect her. I have watched as her family's ministry has developed and expanded in new directions. Her response has always been gracious, even when she might have felt uncomfortable. I asked Lorna to share her story as a Christian woman and a pastor's wife. Much of the content comes from a talk she gave several years ago. Though her message was given to a group of pastors' wives, its wisdom and truths are for any Christian woman whether married or not; it will apply universally, because we are all "women in Christ."

Lorna sees herself as a person "created for commitment," first to God and His work, then to her husband and family. She believes her call is unique because it is a call to minister to the pastor, as his wife. (Wouldn't we *all* be better off if we accepted our calls — whether it is to a husband, family, single, ministry or job?) Lorna has done this with dedication and commitment.

Lorna met her husband, Ron, in the fourth grade. He was a newcomer to her school, and every girl in the fourth and fifth grade had a crush on him. She remembers spelling out the words "I love you" to him, a message she has never given to any other man besides her father and three sons. At the time, Lorna did not intend to marry a pastor, but she sees now there were clues about what was to come. As a young married couple, the pastor of their church always asked Ron for help when he needed a teacher or speaker. Ron was always ready and available for he loved to study and teach the Word of God.

One day, after ten years of marriage and three children, Ron told Lorna he believed God was calling him into full-time ministry. Lorna recognized immediately the leap of faith this would require; they would need to sell their home and relocate so that Ron could attend seminary. It also set up daunting financial challenges.

The next morning, Lorna cried as soon as she was alone, overcome with anxiety as she considered how these changes could affect her family. Later in the day the Spirit of God began to calm Lorna's fears, and by that evening she was ready to go meet the challenge. Both she and Ron were now convinced that God had placed a call on their lives. The journey began.

Now over thirty years later, she listens to her husband preach with greater passion and discernment than he had years before. Their boys are grown and have their own families, so she sits by herself on the front pew. It is the place she has resided for many years, by his side, before he goes to the pulpit to preach.

It hasn't been an easy life. They faced years of trials, despair and loneliness. But there have been years of triumphs and encouragement from patient, godly people. At times the harsh criticisms from disgruntled church members made Pastor Ron want to quit his ministry and get a different job. Happily, these thoughts would quickly pass. Each of life's lessons, whether they become a failure or success, will result in a memory and a milestone.

As Lorna reflects on some memories, she recalls a couple that was ready to quit their marriage because of their many differences and insensitivities. They were simply tired of trying. That was ten years ago. The same couple now sits together in church, holding each other's hands and listening intently to the sermon.

Lorna also sees many teenagers in the service, carefully taking notes as her husband preaches. Many of them she has known as squirmy children and is grateful for the privilege to have watched them mature both physically and spiritually. It reminds her of a special family she and Ron loved and nurtured for several years. The family no longer attends church, and she sometimes wonders what must have been said or done to offend them. Perhaps she will never know why they left. Worse than not knowing, she sometimes hears painful reports of angry gossip against the church and Pastor Ron.

Still, such heartache cannot get in the way of her commitment to obey her calling. Lorna is able to worship and serve with Christian brothers and sisters who love them deeply in Christ. As they get older, the Holy Spirit drives them to persevere. God has given them purpose and humble dependence upon Him for strength to serve Him and His people. Even so, Lorna is beginning to anticipate meeting Jesus face-to-face, and the sense that her time is running out spurs her passions.

Both Lorna and Ron desire to leave a legacy of faithfulness to each other, their family, and to the body of Christ. They pray continually for wisdom, strength and faithfulness to God.

In a recent book called *A Handbook for Minister's Wives,* Dorothy Kelly Patterson discusses the challenging role of being married to a pastor. Along with the importance of a strong commitment to personal Christian character and conduct, a growing personal relationship with Christ is cornerstone, or key, to this ministry. After all, it is the foundation for influence on their family, acquaintances and the body of Christ. Pastor's wives have within their power the ability to enhance or destroy their husband's work.

This is a true principle for all married women.

Lorna stresses that a pastor's wife is graced by God to do a unique work of ministry. Such a woman faces enormous expectations that come from many directions. Lorna says, "We are expected to blend in, head up many programs, show enthusiasm and display abounding energy to serve in every ministry possible."

A pastor's wife lives with complicated relationships. First, there are never ending demands to raise well-behaved children. Lorna can also describe what it is like to experience a husband's disappointments, suffer with his defeats, shoulder his pressures and serve as chief analysts of his sermons and plans. A pastor's wife is discouraged from getting involved in conflicts regarding church leadership, yet she is often treated as part of the problem. She may even be shunned. "Sometimes it is like we are chameleons," Lorna says, "showing and living out the right color to meet each expectation with grace." Many times, a pastor will be judged by his wife's visible character and Christ-like qualities. If these are in question, her husband's ministry will suffer and possibly fail.

"As the 'first lady' of the church," Lorna says, "my relationship with my husband puts me in a vulnerable position. Many churches place upon the pastor's wife expectations that are not biblically supported." Trying to meet the human traditions and pre-conceived ideas of what a pastor and his family should be like might feel like living in a house of glass. "However, like all believers, we are not under the scrutiny of the local body but under the scrutiny of the Word of God." Still, Lorna admits that sometimes she and Ron wonder, "Will the people love us, protect us and nurture us as they would other church members?"

"Pastors' wives share their lives with the church congregation, their respective families, friends and those in their sphere of influence. Pray for God's wisdom, for He desires to lavish His good and perfect gifts on all of us. God desires to fulfill our roles, which pleases Him, but we must trust He will do it."

As Lorna honors the Lord and enhances her husband's effectiveness, she may only receive accolades from a few. But she knows that if she honors God by obeying his call for her commitment, He is pleased. Lorna looks to Scripture for encouragement. The Bible speaks about womanly character and conduct in 1 Timothy 2:2-7 and 3:11. She also reminds herself why God created women in the first place from Genesis 2:20. She is to be a helper to Ron. Lorna believes the role and function for all women is special and given to us by God for His good purposes.

Lorna has learned the importance of monitoring her words, attitudes and actions. From her personal study of the Bible and her efforts to live in the way it teaches, she understands that she must first submit herself to God and then look to take care of Ron as best she can. For Lorna, this includes having good communication and being physically available to him. She also wants to provide a home for him where Christ is seen, a quiet spirit is evident and strong convictions are conveyed. Such an environment creates a foundation of trust and peace, which benefits both their marriage relationship and their ministry.

She believes every Christian woman ultimately has the same ministry — to be a gracious woman in Christ. The application of such a responsibility takes place both inside and out. Titus 2:3-5 describes a woman's personal responsibility to grow in godly character and cultivate healthy relationships. The passage in 1 Peter 3 advises women to *"...let not your adornment be merely external... but let it be the hidden person of the heart, with the imperish-*

able quality of a gentle and quiet spirit, which is precious in the sight of God" (Italics Mine). This passage teaches women about their conduct, attitude and dress. When this directive is implemented women honor their God and His desire for them. As Lorna integrated these concepts into her daily life, she senses the fulfillment of living to please God in all areas of her life. Oh, that all His women could be able to say this. Sad thing is we can when we follow His Word.

Are you as drawn into Lorna's life as I am? Her example of commitment to the Biblical role of being God's woman, then as a pastor's wife and mother — spurs me to live a life implementing the same diligence as my Lord's woman. Once again, Lorna serves as an example not only to pastor's wives, but to all women that they, too, can influence others through their example of love, encouragement and prayer. When women willingly occupy the role set down for them by the very God who created them, they fulfill their purpose and bring Him honor.

What has God called *you* to? Have you followed through with His calling?

After Thoughts

Together, you and I have explored the lives of several women. One woman was once incapacitated by fear, but now walks shoulder to shoulder with her mate in a camp ministry. Two women raised in false religious systems discovered the truth of Jesus Christ and His plans for their lives. Another found out her value came not from her appearance or having a boyfriend but from the unique way God designed her. All of the women have overcome obstacles and heartache. All of them have looked to God to be the woman He desires. They have my deepest respect, love and admiration.

Truthfully, no woman was ever created by God as an after-thought. No woman is second-class in His eyes. No. He has woven each one, shaped each one and called each one. The ladies I have written about have looked to God's calling, and with that calling, their lives provided the opportunity for great influence; influence that permeates the living of the souls within their midst.

Before you close the pages of this book take some time to consider the following:

What woman — or women — have you influenced throughout your life?

How were they influenced?

Who do you know today who could be impacted by your legacy?

How has studying God's word — the Bible — changed your mind, heart and life?

Do you see God at work in you as you live? Has He transformed your life at home or at work? What about your family relationships? How about within your church fellowship?

Does anything prevent you from maximizing all God has intended for you?

Is the God who created and saved you too impotent to work through you?

Here is my challenge to you. Every morning as you wake up, make a decision about whom you will serve that day. Be a Joshua; commit your day, time, energy and heart to follow and serve Him alone. Let your choice affect your actions, your words, your appearance, your investments of time. When you find yourself in a frustrating day, do yourself a favor and seek God in prayer. Ask Him for wisdom and help. As a wonderful woman in the Lord, you are to be His permeating influence in the world around you. You won't be sorry, and He will be pleased.

As you have been reading about these women and their relationships with God it may be that you wonder how you, too, can go through the process of becoming His. I believe with all my heart that we were created for fellowship with the sovereign God; the Bible tells us so! The following can help you begin or begin again.

God offers us a free gift — the ability to have a relationship with Him now and go to Heaven to be with Him when we die. On our own, we do things that are wrong and this separates us from Him. There is nothing we could ever do to be good enough or to make up for all our offenses. In spite of this, God loves us so much that He sent His son, Jesus, to take the punishment we deserved. All we have to do is accept it.

1. Accepting God's gift of salvation is to **admit** that we have failed to meet His standards. By admitting our sin, we find that we are separated from Him. *"For the wages of sin is death* (eternal separation)*, but the free gift of God is eternal life in Christ Jesus our Lord"* (Romans 6:23, Italics mine).

2. Accepting God's gift involves putting your **trust** in Jesus Christ and not yourself. Jesus lived a perfect life, was crucified on a cross, and came back to life after three days. *"But as many as received Him, to them He gave*

the right to become the children of God, to those who believe in His name" (John 1:12, Italics mine).

If you choose to take this important step read the following verses (John 3:16; Acts 4:12, 16:31; Romans 3:23, 5:8, 6:23). Here is a simple prayer to help you talk to God from your heart. Please know it is not this prayer that saves you, but the belief that led you to pray… something like:

Dear God, I admit I am a sinner and I now understand that my sin separates me from you. I believe that Jesus, being God, paid the penalty for all my sins when He died on the cross and rose again from the dead. I want to place my trust in Him as my Savior and Lord. Thank you for this generous gift of love and forgiveness and the promise of eternal life with you when I die.

Your search to be clean and to be free of the burden of sin is a choice you must make. One day every person will come before the living God to give an account for his or her life, choices and words (Galatians 4:4,5; Ephesians 1:5,13). The group that rejects Jesus' gift will spend eternity separated from God, and ushered, by their own volition, to Hell. Those who accept Jesus' gift will receive rewards and be ushered into Heaven to be forever with their Savior, Lord and God. I pray you are part of the second group.

If you have made the decision to accept God's gift, tell someone! Become a part of a Bible-believing church so that you can mature through the Word of God. May God make Himself known to you as you seek His face!

Ellen's gift of exhortation has been a source of great encouragement to our church. In *Designed by the Master*, women will see how other sisters in Christ found strength to cope and overcome in the face of various difficult life situations. The Gospel and the Word of God are lifted up as the balm for a wounded life, the key ingredients necessary for healing. I pray that you will be blessed as you read.

Justin Greene, Senior Pastor of Salem
Heights Church

In *Designed by the Master,* Ellen Jacobs brings wisdom and many life experiences as she pens the words of this moving book. As she shares the lives of women, her insight is not only touching but also encouraging to the reader. The transforming power of God shines through as each woman's story is told. I recommend that women of all ages read this book. Ellen has been a Godly example in my life, and I am thankful for the years we have served together.

Ron Schafer, STEPS Ministry and church planting; Retired Senior Pastor, Salem Heights Church

Designed by the Master: Women of Permeating Influence shares the lives of women changed by an intense relationship with Jesus Christ. Each woman's story honestly explores her journey to find the incredible love, acceptance and motivation of a Divine Savior. Though all the women begin with their own struggle — abuse, divorce, eating disorders, sexual promiscuity and other hurtful behaviors — each becomes a godly, influential woman in Jesus Christ. Jacobs' book reveals the potential of every woman in Christ and is a must-read for those who work with them.

Deborah Hedstrom-Page, author, pastor's wife, and teacher.

I have known Ellen for many years and admire her heart for women in pain. As Ellen shares her life story in this book it will minister to those who can relate to her life. The stories of those who have impacted her life also are powerful expressions of God's ability to make beauty from ashes.

Anne Jeffers, Women's Ministries professor, Corban College

Ellen is a remarkable woman whose life has been used by God to minister to women for several decades. She is a person with many loves. They include her love for Jesus Christ, God's Word, and just about every person she has ever met. After her husband's death, Ellen pursued an education, which has only added to her ability to love and serve men and women through teaching and counseling. To know Ellen is to know the loves of her life. The rich accounts in this book will bless and strengthen readers to continue fulfilling God's mission, trusting Him for grace and wisdom.

Dr. Rich Meyers, Psychology professor,

Corban College

The gripping life stories intertwined with biblical principles in this book will be helpful to all, especially to those who have experienced similar situations in life. It is a good read. I recommend it as a guide to helping all of us realize the individual design God has for our lives and how we impact others in our sphere of influence. Ellen Jacobs has interwoven her many years of counseling experience throughout the message of the book.

Reno Hoff, President, Corban College & Graduate School

Breinigsville, PA USA
22 February 2010
232970BV00001B/2/P

9 781607 916895